TERRENCE WOOD

MW01224112

BEFORE YOU
GO PRO

A STORY WITHIN A MULTI-BILLION
DOLLAR INDUSTRY

outskirtspress
DENVER, COLORADO

Before You Go Pro
A Story Within a Multi-Billion Dollar Industry
All Rights Reserved.
Copyright © 2014 Terrence Wood
V3.0 R2.0

Outskirts Press, Inc.
http://www.outskirtspress.com

ISBN: 978-1-4787-2276-2

Outskirts Press and the "OP" logo are trademarks belonging to Outskirts Press, Inc.

PRINTED IN THE UNITED STATES OF AMERICA

This book is dedicated to my grandfather, Willie Wood, who put his body on the line for the game of football and inspired my career. To my parents, who kindled my passion for the love of football. To my loving wife and kids, who have allowed me the time to pursue this labor of love, and have whole-heartedly supported Before You Go Pro. And last but not least, I dedicate this book to all of the aspiring football players across the country. May your journey be one of health, growth, and true triumph!

Special Thanks to Blessings Robertson-Winn, Antoinette Bobbit, Dale Dickson, Victoria Jones, Victor Rogers, Donald Strickland, Cedric Cormier, the Criswell family, and all of our Kickstarter supporters.

God bless!

Contents

Introduction: The Dream

THE DAY I saw my grandfather, Willie Wood, on stage receiving that gold blazer upon his shoulders, was the day I decided what I wanted to do with the rest of my life! Considering that I was only 9 years old, this was a feat in itself. Nevertheless, at that particular moment I was convinced that I was going to be a professional football player.

However, my grandfather was not just getting any old jacket; he was receiving the jacket of ultimate respect, the jacket of champions, and the jacket of the National Football League Hall of Fame.

"Wow!" I thought, as I watched the elated fans applaud my grandfather's accomplishments. As my grandfather approached the podium, taking in the moment and preparing for his induction speech, I remember thinking, "this is where I am supposed to be. This was intended for me to witness today." And just like that, my mind was made up.

Now I had a mission to accomplish. Not only a mission, a destiny! The NFL was the only option for me, and I was willing to do whatever it took to make it a reality. Just like thousands of other kids throughout the country, football totally consumed me at a young age. It's absolutely amazing how a simple game can produce so much passion, emotion, and excitement in people. The game of football has officially moved ahead of baseball to become America's most popular sport, and Monday Night Football has become our nations most highly rated weekly television program. The peak of football's popularity was, the 2012 Super Bowl, which broke records as the most watched television program in U.S. television history, with an estimated 166.8 million viewers, according to Wikipedia. So of course, with the overwhelming fan hysteria and exposure, comes a boatload of cash for players! Cash that everyone desperately wants to capitalize on.

As for myself, I have always loved football. But there was much more than dollar signs in it for me; there was also honor. The sport had consumed me at such a young age, that I never really realized there was significant money to be made in football until I was about 12 years old. I loved the sport itself, the recognition, and the praise that you received from being good at it. And there were no other options for me but to be good at football.

Later on, the icing on the cake of my career would be my name in bold, on the back of my jersey, the last name of one of the greatest defensive backs to ever grace the grass of an NFL football field. WOOD!

Interesting information quickly passes through crowds, and the football audience is no exception. Throughout my career, my grandfather's legacy was constantly projected on my performance in the game. The expectation of greatness weighed heavily on my shoulders. Fortunately, I was blessed with natural ability: good hands, good speed and good work ethic. But anyone who's ever played a sport is aware that it takes more than just talent to become good at something like football. The physical requirements of the game are obvious, but many people underestimate the mental factors that take place in football. It's chess, not checkers.

Knowing this, I began to pay my dues from a very young age. This meant countless hours studying hundreds of football games, plus reading dozens of football magazines, that I'd beg my mother to buy for me at the checkout line of the grocery store. I was committed to seeing my dream come to fruition, and so was my family.

My father, Andre Wood, was just as passionate about the game as I was. In a way, he was living his gridiron dreams through me. Talented in his own right, my father ended his career after a couple of stellar seasons playing semi-pro football, and a training camp opportunity with the Oakland Invaders, of the now defunct USFL league. Once my dad passed the baton to me, it was only natural for him to be passionate about my career. Once I confirmed that my mission was to be in the NFL, my father's passion went into overdrive.

I would have constant practice outside of regular team practice and endless mental preparation about the game of football. Dad and I never casually watched football games. We studied them. My dad instilled in me that I was capable of making it to the top— even though the odds were against me— as long as I was willing to work at it. Being so young, I have to admit I was naive about the amount of preparation ahead for me to succeed in football. I didn't mind the hard work. I'm not saying I loved every push-up or every wind sprint. What I did love was the *payoff*. And, my path to football super-stardom began with little league football, playing for the San Bruno Rams.

It's crazy to watch the evolution of little boys first struggling to put on their uniform, to their transformation into multi-million dollar investments. Yes! Players are investments—for families, schools, corporations and NFL team owners. But, for the player it's important not to lose sight of why he plays the game. The best advice I can give to a young player is to always make sure he is playing for the love of the game. While that may seem obvious to a player who's still a kid, it becomes extremely difficult to remember as a player climbs higher up the ladder of football success.

This book is intended for the kids, and the parents/guardians who venture into the world of football. My aim is to give a behind-the-scenes look at the laughter, the tears, the successes, and the disappointments that were scenes within my journey. My perspective of the game morphed throughout my 19 years of experience on the field. The game of football has afforded me, and my family amazing opportunities. It also came with huge sacrifices and losses. Just remember, anything worth having is worth working hard for. Knowing this now, I look at it as my duty and honor to share with you, whether you are a youth player, a parent, or just a lover of football, what you need to know "Before You Go Pro".

CHAPTER 1

The Business of Football

FOR EVERYONE WHO doesn't know, the business of football begins in high school! High school is the first time young football players begin to get looked at as potential dollar signs. This is the first time tangible dollars can become attached to a kids name in the form of a college scholarship. Every year, college football programs throughout the country sift through high schools across the country with the intent to find and woo young football talent. If you want to compete in the world of big time college football, it is essential that your program is a competitor in college football's second season, better known as the "recruiting season".

Football always has and always will be about winning games. Every college program knows that in order to have more check marks in the "wins" column, as opposed to the "losses" column, its team needs talent! The great thing about college football is that there is absolutely no limit to how many great players can be on one particular team. For example, take the University of Miami, did you know that at one time their football program was blessed with a running back surplus that consisted of greats like Clinton Portis, Willis McGahee, and Frank Gore? All of whom have been considered upper echelon NFL running backs within the last decade! These guys were on the same college depth chart competing day after day with each other for any chance of playing time they could possibly get their hands on. There is not an NFL team in the League that would not love to have all three men in the backfield during their prime. It's ironic how college football has gotten to the point where one team's third string tailback could end up being an NFL team's Pro Bowl running back one day. This clearly illustrates the fact that the more talent you have, the better the team. And the better the team, the stronger the program, and guess what follows next? Cha-Ch'ing! The cash register.

Year after year, you will find a direct correlation between the teams in the national championship hunt and the teams who produce the greatest recruiting classes. For example, according to Rivals.com, the list of schools that finished among the top eight in 2013 for football recruiting, included:

1) **Alabama**
2) **Ohio St.**
3) **Notre Dame**
4) **Florida**
5) **Michigan**
6) **LSU**
7) **Ole Miss**
8) **Auburn**

So it should be no surprise that the last seven college football national championships have gone to schools on that list. Schools like Alabama, USC, and Ohio State never rebuild their programs; they just reload their programs. The old saying "It takes money to make money" has never been more evident than it is now in college football. Year after year, as top-flight programs battle for big-time high school and junior college recruits, there has been an increase in pressure for athletic departments to upgrade the playing environment for their teams. Facilities are marketing tools for schools to bait the players they need to win. In turn wins are increased by securing top talent. Top talent leads financial donors to the athletic department of the university. This is cash flow that many universities rely on to operate year after year.

College football recruiting is like a military arms race and everyone is fighting for the big guns. When college-bound players research where to play, believe me, facilities are one of the things consistently at the top of their list. It's no coincidence that the best college football programs have some of the most impressive facilities. According to the Chronicle of Higher Education, from 2002 to 2007, schools in the nation's six premier athletic conferences at that time raised at least $3.9 billion for stadium expansions, weight rooms and new practice facilities. For the powerhouse programs, the money raised is an investment to ensure future success. Other universities that have lacked the wow factor for years are quickly catching on. Take Oklahoma State. After receiving a generous $165 million contribution from Alum, T. Boone Pickens, the Oklahoma State Cowboys now have the missing "bling" factor needed to strengthen their program. In 2011, the Oklahoma State Cowboys were one game away from playing in the national championship game, after years of being a Big XII and Big 8 doormat.

How can a school like San Jose State or Florida International ever expect to battle with the likes of the University of Florida, or USC? When you look at the benefits the powerhouse schools can offer a kid, compared to some of the lower market schools, the comparison is night and day. The University of Florida has donors who contribute in one year what Florida International has been trying to raise for nearly a decade.

There is NO comparison! Just ask coach Jeff Tedford, recently replaced at Cal-Berkeley, who was responsible for turning that program into a very competitive team in the PAC-12 Conference. After suffering years of humiliation as one of the PAC-10 Conference bottom dwellers, Cal put together nine consecutive winning seasons during Tedford's tenure. Despite the amazing turnaround coach Tedford accomplished with the program, he was the first one to admit that there was still more work to be done. To go from consecutive winning seasons to a perennial national championship contender, the Cal football facilities were in need of a little cosmetic surgery, specifically in the form of a new state-of-the-art training facility for its players.

Top athletes want to win ball games, and the most visible way for a University to show an athlete that winning is important is by putting money into their facilities. Young super-star athletes like Cal alums, Aaron Rodgers and Marshawn Lynch, have to feel like a school can provide them with all of the tools necessary to accomplish their athletic goals. Coach Tedford, during his time at Cal, showed the higher-ups how attractive and financially lucrative having a great football program could be. As a result, the decision makers at UC Berkeley agreed to abide by college football's new rules, and now, Cal has a NEW $150 million athletic facility, and a NEW state of the art football stadium. Now Cal's new head football coach, Sonny Dykes, will be able to fully engage in the college football "arms race" that goes on every year for our nation's top young athletes. But it's a race that changes constantly. As I write, the University of Oregon's new facility, funded by Nike owner Phil Knight, has every other athletic facility playing second fiddle.

College football stadiums and athletic facilities evolve like new cell phones, making the stage that these kids play on, even more grand. For the purpose of a comparison, I will point out that the size of the NFL's largest stadium is Fed Ex Field, home of the Washington Redskins, with a seating capacity of 85,000 people. However, if the Redskins' home were compared to the college ranks, Fed Ex Field would only be considered the fifteenth largest college stadium in terms of seating capacity. For NFL bound athletes coming out of schools like Michigan, Penn State, and Tennessee, going pro is actually taking a step backwards in terms of the number of people they are used to performing in front of. The entertainment platform of college football, to a certain degree, is setting the standard for athletic entertainment across the board, and every college football program desperately wants to keep up!

CHAPTER 2

Investments in Cleats

THE COLLEGE RECRUITING process will feel like one of the best times of a player's entire life. When I think back on my recruiting experience, it really was one of the best times of my life! It's exciting to have colleges tell you how much they love you and what a great player you are. It feels like all of the hard work has been paid off in full. The recruiting process is also the first indication of how football can quickly start to become more business than sport. Which is totally okay, if you are prepared to do business. You have to be your best advocate on and off the field. You must be aware of your value, your strengths, your weaknesses, and be ready to market your gift in the best way.

As a player, you should know that every year college football programs across the country make lists of the prospective student athletes they are targeting to recruit. Now someone might ask, "how do the schools come up with their list?" Or, "how can I be one of the targeted prospects?" Good question!

The answer is that there are high school recruiting publications, Internet sites, television shows and summer camps that help some of the top college football programs generate their prospective lists. As long as a young athlete is consistently making plays on the field in his hometown, chances are someone will be watching.

This is especially true if the competition and talent level happens to be excellent in that particular player's area. Consider Los Angeles, Houston,

Dallas, and Miami, to name a few. These cities have developed reputations for turning out great talent, and as such, have been labeled, "recruiting hotbeds". Understandably, top-notch college football programs direct the majority of their recruiting efforts in these zones. The odds of finding great players are always higher when searching through an area that is ripe with talent. These hotbeds produce athletes that tend to be more battle-tested because the standard of competition is so high.

The recruiting competition is also very high because everyone is fishing in the same ponds. It's no wonder large annual budgets are created to woo players into college programs. Even if the budgets have been depleted, schools will still find the funds to snag the right player. The private plane trips, women, and cash are not the tactics used to lure every recruit. But all of these tactics and more have been used to lure the right recruit. It's just considered old-fashioned incentive.

As a player, excuse me, I mean as a *commodity*, you have to be aware when the game becomes a business. Believe me, that's how these football programs look at it. The higher your player ranking, the more you are heavily pursued. Again, college football recruiting is literally like an old fashioned arms race. The objective of a college coach/recruiter is to load their team up with as many gifted football players as they possibly can in order to obliterate the competition. Just ask Pete Carroll, former head coach of the USC fighting Trojans. AKA: Tailback "U." Carroll went into the 2007 season with a depth chart comprised of 10 tailbacks (many of whom were highly-touted ball carriers coming out of high school). Since there is no team limit on how many Reggie Bush's or Adrian Petersons you can have, some schools take no chances and stack their team with an overload of big-time recruits. The more investment in attracting the top players, the more profit generated for the university in the long run.

It's estimated that the University of Notre Dame rakes in around $15 million dollars annually by granting NBC the rights to televise Notre Dame's home games. That paper alone is enough incentive to put a quality "product" on the field. Many of the recruiting gurus, such as *Rivals.com* and *Scout.com*, rank their overall top-300 high school prospects, and also rank players from across the country, by individual positions. So it's typical that top players in the country receive scholarship offers from many different schools. And as a player, that's what you want. Options!

You want options to go to whatever school you desire, instead of settling for whatever school you can get. As a potential prospect, your job is to make your name well known. The best place to start to develop a name for yourself is with your local daily newspaper (which is probably online). Also, many kids make a name for themselves at many of the various recruiting combines, or 7-on-7 tournaments hosted across the country.

With the thousands of dollars I see some recruits' families pay, to increase their kids' exposure, utilizing the local press can prove to be an economically wise calling card. Just imagine if your picture is always on the front page of the sports section or regularly on the local television news after the weekend's high school games. College coaches don't just scan the high school section of the newspaper and related websites because they want to. They have to. It's their trade. Picture Urban Meyer, the head football coach of the Ohio State Buckeyes, picking up the paper, watching the nightly news, and always seeing your face, and hearing people rave about your talent on the field. Naturally, he is going to be interested. He's a football coach! So remember, keep your name in the local press. There shouldn't be a fall weekend that goes by without your name appearing somewhere locally.

Some high schools have a reputation for putting out quality players, so college programs will constantly send out questionnaires to these schools, to get the head coach's opinion of the players on his team, along with players from the opposing teams on their schedule. It's essential that as a young player you stay in good graces with your high school coaching staff during your recruiting process. Remember, negative comments get around twice as fast as positive ones. It is essential to protect yourself from negative labels, *as they can last you your whole career!*

Colleges send out thousands of recruiting letters a year, but they only have an average of 16 to 24 football scholarships available annually. The number of scholarships available largely depends on the number of senior graduates, dropouts, and NFL entries a particular team has. Do the math, and you will see that many prospects are weeded out for various reasons from the thousands initially pursued! There's a thick stack of hay to rake through before offers can be put on the table.

For me, it quickly became evident that I needed to make my mark on the football field in my junior year of high school. I knew that many of the upper echelon recruits, who were recruited by big-time schools, already had offers rolling in after their junior season. That was over ten years ago. In today's recruiting world, the best players begin receiving offers after their sophomore season, and most have already made verbal commitments to schools before they even hit the field their senior year. There has even been news of kids receiving college football offers, as early as eighth grade!

This gives you a little glimpse into just how far in advance some of these universities plan their programs out. Many of the top college programs run their teams identically to Fortune 500 companies. If your head coach is managing a multi-million dollar contract, then isn't he the equivalent of a high level CEO? At the end of every college football season, everyone is graded. Everyone from the head coach to the equipment manager is evaluated and held accountable for his performance, and his capacity to improve his particular performance. If there is no capacity for improvement, then athletic directors will look for replacements. The demand and expectation of greatness is at a high level across the board.

Players are also evaluated, and their performance dictates how a coach will prioritize the positions his staff needs to recruit. Recruiting is a priority, and coaches go hard to improve their team for the next season. If a team is unfortunately last in pass defense, then I guarantee there will be heavy emphasis on recruiting junior college and high school defensive backs to fill that immediate need.

Nevertheless, if there is a bright and promising star outside the team's immediate need, they will not pass on the opportunity to secure him. Some of the top players will receive scholarship offers from just about every school because they are just that *good*! If there is an opportunity to get a Randy Moss type player, it doesn't matter if your team doesn't have the need for a wide receiver that year, every school that touts itself as worthy will still try to recruit a Randy Moss. But the majority of high school players and junior college players will only be recruited by a select number of colleges that are really focused on filling holes for certain positions.

For me, after a pretty successful junior year, it became evident that there was a great divide between my options: There were schools that were somewhat interested, and others that were definitely interested. I had received recruiting letters from just about every school anyone could think of (Michigan State, Nebraska, Florida, Oklahoma, and the University of Georgia to name a few.) Oddly enough, none of those schools gave me a call. As it turned out, I was just one of thousands of prospects on their mailing lists, and letters were just the first step in the recruiting process.

The second step is when a school takes the time during the recruitment of a prospect to request a player's film. Schools may view the film online through a recruiting service, or request it directly from the athlete's high school or junior college. But all the college scouts will definitely want to see film. Some coaches may begin calling your house at what's referred to as "the legal time." The NCAA (National Collegiate Athletic Association) actually has rules on when it's appropriate for universities to call prospects. Even though many coaches try to find loopholes around the rules, especially with the emergence of text messages and social networking, but the rules are firm (check the NCAA Clearing House Recruiting Rule Book for more details).

The first school to ever dial my telephone number was the University of Virginia. And Oregon, Colorado, Hawaii and Arizona State were not far behind. It is **extremely** important for anyone serious about receiving a college scholarship to understand how recruiting works. Like I said before, these programs have a specific amount of money they dedicate towards recruiting. Since these schools run like top-level corporations, they answer to the powers that be if they misspend their money.

Here is why this is important to you as a potential prospect, parent, or guardian of a prospect: You can tell how much interest a university has in you by the amount of money it is willing to spend on you. Now don't get me wrong. Letters from university football programs are great. But it's not going to break any team's recruiting budget just to send you a letter across the country.

During my recruiting process, my family and I made a *big* mistake because we missed some key indicators of interest. Hopefully, you will learn from this mistake and not make the same one.

The University of Virginia was not only the first school to call my house, but also the most aggressive in pursuing me. They sent their recruiting coordinator out to visit me my junior year in high school to simply express interest on behalf of the school. Now that's what you would consider dipping into the recruiting budget a little bit! UVA showed two key indicators of major interest, which were overlooked by my family and me. From their flying cross-country to visit me my junior year, to being the first school to call me at the legal time going into my senior season, UVA was saying that I was highly valued by their coaching staff as a recruit. While there are no guarantees in college football recruiting, the team that shows you the most interest in terms of dollars and timing is definitely a team that warrants your undivided attention. That's not to say the attention from the University of Virginia coaching staff went unnoticed by my family and me, because it didn't. But I will say we did not put as much weight on Virginia's advances towards me as we should have!

Being oblivious to the negotiating tactics, and being clueless when you are entering into levels of serious business can create a faulty environment for your decision- making process. While college ball may appear on the outside to be just a game, it is important that you realize you are engaging in *big business*. If you change your perspective from being one of an inexperienced novice, to that of a knowledgeable, well-read, and business-minded athlete, your chances of success are greatly increased because you are making informed decisions.

CHAPTER 3

First Class Treatment

AS I WATCHED the final seconds countdown on the scoreboard, I found myself getting more excited. It was the final game of my high school career, and once again, my team failed to make it to the playoffs. For many of my teammates, it was the end of an era; the last time they would ever wear shoulder pads and a helmet again. But I was excited because I knew I had something to look forward to after this game. In my mind, my football career was just *beginning*. Soon, I would be on a flight to experience my very first recruiting trip.

I must admit my idea of a recruiting trip was far from what I actually experienced. In the eyes of a 17-year-old boy, it was beyond my wildest dreams! You have to keep in mind that a recruiting trip is like a glorified first date. The school's job is to try everything within its means to make you never want to leave their campus. The more talented you are, the harder they will try!

The first recruiting trip I took was to the University of Virginia. As a prospect from California, it was a pretty big deal. My Hall of Fame grandfather, Willie Wood, decided to tag along for the trip, given he lived nearby in Washington, D.C. Me and my father agreed to meet my grandfather in Washington, D.C then take the two hour car ride to Charlottesville, Virginia. This was the first step toward realizing my dream. After years of hearing about other prospects and their recruiting experiences, I found myself actually living mine out loud. What once was mental visualization and years of self-prophecy was now my physical reality.

When we arrived on campus, we met with coach Danny Wilmer, the University of Virginia recruiting specialist. He was responsible for acquiring names like Thomas Jones and the infamous "Barber Twins" (Tiki and Ronde) to play ball at Virginia. Coach Wilmer had a bright smile on his face as he greeted us, the type of smile that made me feel like he had been waiting all day to see me. The hotel I stayed at was elaborately decorated with Virginia Cavalier football signs and memorabilia. There was also a huge welcome banner behind the front desk. The receptionist also carried the same smile on her face as coach Wilmer, but hers was a lot cuter, of course. This was first-class treatment, something I had never experienced before, but I could definitely get used to.

After the small talk, coach Wilmer asked if we were hungry. We definitely were, so we went to a place that catered to students to grab a bite. The place was pretty much empty, except for a couple of student athletes. I was amazed by the amount of food the cooks were trying to put on my plate. I was not even in the program yet, and they were already trying to beef me up! After lunch, it was time to meet up with my "player host".

Every school pairs recruits up with a current player that they feel will be a good personality fit. I guess they figure it will improve the schools chances of getting that particular prospect to commit. At the University of Virginia, my player host was a guy who happened to be a freshman defensive back. He was the logical choice to be my host because not only did we play the same position, he coincidentally was the only player on Virginia's roster who was also from the West Coast. Let's call this player David, for the purpose of anonymity.

Once I met up with "D" he made it very well known that he planned to get me so intoxicated that I'd have a tough time remembering my own name, let alone what was about to go down that night. These weren't the first words I expected to hear coming out of a division 1A football player's mouth, but I definitely went along with the game plan. In fact, David had a whole itinerary planned for the night, which included about four different house/dorm parties.

Contrary to the intended plan however, I do remember a little bit of that night, and I had a damn good time. There was a common theme with every party we attended. Each one was stocked with plenty of alcohol and equally stocked with plenty of college women. Drinking alcohol was not something I indulged in at the time, so it didn't take long at all for the alcohol to start to influence me. As soon as we would start to get settled in at one party, David would grab me off the couch and we'd be on to the next party. After a few more drinks I was so intoxicated I didn't give a damn where I was anymore. The last thing I remember was waking up in David's dorm room, on his bed, with two college women talking about how cute I was while caressing my head.

I remember being dumbfounded by the number of women I met who had very wealthy families and were not afraid to let you know it. Many were from families with big oil money or political money. They were all calling me "Cali Boy" and made it known that I would be well taken care of if I came to play ball for their beloved Virginia Cavaliers. Of course I told them I was coming!

In a borrowed car of a teammate, David drove me back to my hotel where he assisted me as I stumbled back to my hotel room. Lying wounded, but in full glory, David stared down at me as I fell on my bed. He emphatically stressed that I had better sober up and rest. (I had to recover quickly to attend an early morning breakfast meeting with coach Wilmer.) More importantly, he added, we had an even bigger night of partying coming up tomorrow. It was as if David took pride in this type of social conditioning.

As intoxicated as I was, David could have left me in the hotel lobby and I would have slept just fine. It's ridiculous that the possible consequences of our actions never entered my mind or David's. As my head hit the pillow that night, I couldn't believe the night I just experienced. This was only the first night of my first recruiting trip, but I already felt ready to commit to Virginia. The topper was that I still had an extra night of paradise coming my way!

The next day, I got an 8:30am wakeup call from the front desk. The voice on the other end informed me that coach Wilmer would be downstairs to meet with my father and me at 9:00 am. Still hung over from the night before, I staggered around the room trying to put on my clothes. That's when I realized that not only did I have a *roommate*, but that he had a naked woman in the bed with him! Turns out, it was one of the other recruits.

I desperately tried to recall my actions from the night before. I remember thinking to myself "my girlfriend is going to kill me if she finds out about this!" I threw on my clothes and made my way downstairs slowly, trying my best not to throw up. I was greeted by the bright-eyed and bushy tailed excitement from my father, who was waiting for me in a plush hotel loveseat. Five minutes later, coach Wilmer walked through the door. With great enthusiasm, he gave us the rundown for the day as we ventured off for our tour of the campus. Acting as our tour guide, coach Wilmer did a great job mapping out the university campus and the stellar athletic facilities.

Our first tour of duty was a meeting with coach George Welsh, the head coach of the Virginia Cavaliers. Coach Welsh was well respected for the great turnaround of UVA's program. We entered a team meeting room where we sat face to face with coach Welsh. I couldn't believe I was really sitting down with one of the greatest coaches in big time college football. He quickly made it very clear that the University of Virginia was the place to be. The goal of everyone in the program, he explained, was to win UVA's first National Championship. Then coach Welsh asked me, "Would you like to be a part of something like that?" He knew that my answer was "yes" by the ear-to-ear grin across my face. Once I verbally confirmed what my face had so blatantly communicated, coach Welsh offered me a full-ride scholarship right there on the spot!

I couldn't believe it. I was speechless, yet very eager to respond. He tempered his offer like a well-trained businessman, saying, "Now, I want you to take some time and think about this before you make your decision." The pressure was off, and my heart found its way back into my chest. He finished up with a more in-depth explanation of his business plan and how I could play a part in its realization.

After listening to coach Welsh's vision, we made our way over to the stadium for breakfast. There was a beautiful buffet style layout overlooking the team's magnificent football field. The whole time I found myself gazing out of the window in amazement. All I could do was look at the thousands of seats in the stadium and wonder what it would be like to run out onto the field in front of a packed house. I had never felt so close to touching my dreams as I did that day.

After we ate, we headed downstairs to the game-day locker room. I quickly noted that I had come a long way from the metal wire lockers of Riordan High school, back in San Francisco. Wowed by the professional, wood-finished lockers, I caught the glimmer of something from the corner of my eye. It was a nameplate that read, **"Terrence Wood."** I almost fell through the floor! The locker was decked out with a helmet, pants, cleats, gloves, and a "#1" jersey. The same number that I played with in high school! I was sold! I was ready to throw on the uniform and sign my letter of intent. If I could have, I would have run right out of the locker room and onto the field to simulate my first game-day appearance. I was overflowing with excitement, and coach Wilmer was pleased. This was the stuff that dreams were made of!

The next order of business was a meeting with the academic advisors. While smart kids and their parents actually use academics as a factor in their college decision-making, unfortunately, only a small percentage of football players actually take the academic part of the recruiting trip seriously. Unfortunately, I didn't give academics too much thought. Most athletes want to know what grades they *need* in order to be eligible to play, and that is where they set the bar. Many athletes strive for just enough and nothing more, and it's unfortunate. I was so tired from the night before that I actually had to fight to keep myself from falling asleep while listening to the academic advisor's presentation. All I could focus on was the night ahead of me. And I completely missed out on the fact that my *education* would be the thing to provide me with real options, both on and off the field. This was something I would later come to regret.

My player host, David, picked me up at about 8:00pm, and our first stop was the liquor store. The second stop was back to the dorms to start drinking. That's when I confirmed that the alcohol I drank did not deceive my recollection of the prior night. It was more of the same college debauchery.

I did, however, walk away from the University of Virginia, highly impressed. The team was ranked #12 in the country at the time. The games were always on TV. The playing environment, the social scene, and the student body left no room for any recruit to complain. I remember thinking, what's not to love about UVA? I had also developed a kinship with coach Wilmer, who made an effort to recruit me since I was 16 years old! I flew back to San Francisco the next day, daydreaming of playing football for the Virginia Cavaliers. But what I found out is that those types of dreams usually only last as long as your next recruiting trip, in the world of Big Time College Football!

CHAPTER 4

The University of Colorado

MY NEXT STOP on the recruiting carousel was Boulder, Colorado to visit the #10 ranked Colorado Buffaloes. Since my father went on the Virginia trip with me, my parents decided that my mother should attend the Colorado trip. Now armed with a previous official recruiting trip under my belt, I felt I had a good idea of what to expect. My mother, on the other hand, was oblivious, and for me it was important to keep it that way.

I was extremely excited to go on this trip because Colorado had the youngest head coach in college football. His name was Rick Neuheisel, and he had taken college football by storm. Picture a younger Pete Carroll (former USC coach) all the way up in Colorado, and yes, Neuheisel definitely brought L.A. to the Mountains! Neuheisel had the college football world in the palm of his hand with his exciting offense and well documented recruiting background. The trip was also exciting to me because even though Colorado is in the Midwest, it was highly visible to all the top recruits in California. Their lone Heisman Trophy winner, Rashaan Salaam, was from San Diego.

When I looked over the University of Colorado roster, I was familiar with a handful of the names, given there were kids from my part of northern California already on the team. That was big for me! Compared to the Virginia roster, where there was only one player on the entire team from the west coast. I felt a lot "closer to home" when I was in Colorado.

The college town of Boulder is only about 30 minutes from Denver.

There are four professional sports teams in downtown Denver: Colorado Rockies, Colorado Avalanche, Denver Broncos and the Denver Nuggets. Growing up in Northern California, I rooted for the San Francisco Giants and the 49ers, not to mention the Golden State Warriors, and the San Jose Sharks. So I thought of professional sports teams as synonymous with their cities. For me, Colorado was already shaping up to be right up my alley.

Another important fact was that there were three African American football coaches on the C.U. coaching staff, believe me, the program definitely used that as a selling point to recruit young black athletes. Coach Jon Embree, who eventually ended up becoming the head coach at Colorado (2010-2012), was responsible for recruiting me. When we arrived at the Denver International Airport, he escorted my mother and me into his car and we were off to C.U. I was freezing in the back seat of coach Embree's car. It was December in Colorado, and I quickly tried to recall all of my conversations with coach Embree about the weather in Colorado. That's Right! This guy had sold me on the sun. I remember coach Embree telling me, "The state of Colorado is sunny 300 days of the year, which is more than any in the country". But in my young, 17-year-old mind, I logically assumed someone talking about the sun meant he was also talking about warm weather. Yeah right! As I stared out of his backseat window, I noticed it was certainly sunny, but heaps of snow assured me there'd be no warmth to speak of on this recruiting trip! The snow was piled up as far as my eyes could see.

As we entered Boulder, one thing that definitely stood out was the stadium. Another standout was the two identical large buildings on the right-hand side of the freeway exit. Coach Embree made sure to mention that these buildings were newly built, off-campus co-ed dorms. After spending four years in an all-boys, Catholic high school, the freedom of an off-campus dorm, and the mention of female residents were enough to make my ears stand up.

Five minutes later we pulled up to a four-story structure casually known as Dal Ward. This is the University of Colorado's Athletic Center. Everything to do with athletics, from the athletic director's office, to administrative staff offices, the weight room, training room, game day locker room, meeting rooms, film rooms, cafeteria, computer labs, and academic advisor offices were (and still are), housed in Dal Ward.

The facility was opulent with marble floors throughout the main entry. There were awe-inspiring pictures, murals, and trophies throughout the entire facility. The collection of C.U. memorabilia had my complete attention, and I was inspired by the achievements documented in photos and awards achieved by the Colorado Buffaloes and its coaching staff. Moments frozen in time, such as the "Kordell Stewart to Michael Westbrook" hail-mary at Michigan back in 1994, was just one of the many awe-inspiring visuals at the center. At that moment, I felt someone pat me on the back. I snapped out of my daydream, and saw a familiar face from televised college football games. It was coach A.J. Christoff.

Coach A.J. was an older, veteran coach with an impressive resume prior to his tenure at CU. He had been with Alabama, Georgia Tech, and Notre Dame, and there was no question as to why he was named the team's defensive back coach.

After shaking my mother's hand and a brief introduction, he expressed that he wanted to sit down and have a good talk with me later. Coach A.J.'s energy was sincere and positive. But there was no time to stay and chat. We were on a tight schedule and the next thing on the itinerary was food.

The Cork was the restaurant where all the coaches and recruits were expected to lunch and have a little meet and greet time. This was no ordinary restaurant. The Cork was one of the premier dining spots in all of Colorado. The venue's décor was quite elegant, decked out with linens on the table, crystal stem drinking glasses, and wood-burning fireplaces. The menu confirmed a high-end dining experience with the low-end of steak starting at about $29 dollars. But price was no object tonight, and coach Embree made sure to tell me to order whatever my heart desired. I made sure not to contradict his instruction. As I glanced around the room, I couldn't take my eyes off this big Samoan kid at the table across from me. He was probably the biggest human being I had ever seen in my 17 years of life. The way that he devoured the steak on his plate should have been illegal. He ate it like he was mad at it. I turned to coach Embree and asked, "Is that a recruit?" coach laughed and said, "No! That's Chris Naeole our

All-American left tackle. He will be a first round draft pick this year!" I was thinking, "Man, I see why."

Five minutes later, coach Neuheisel walked into the restaurant. Although we were tucked away in a private dining room at the back of the restaurant, we could all sense him there. He was one of those unique souls blessed with a BIG presence. It was as though the energy in the restaurant had elevated a few notches upon his arrival. His high-wattage smile lit up the room. The program's biggest recruiting weekend was in full swing now with 25 of the nation's finest high school football players in Boulder that weekend. Neuheisel's goal was to close the deal on all of us. In his mind, it was game time!

Known for his great recruiting reputation, coach Neuheisel did not hesitate to start using his charisma and guile to win over the parents in attendance. He walked into the room laughing, giving high fives, shaking hands and working the room like an old pro. As he made his way over to where my mother and I were seated, he introduced himself and sincerely thanked my mother for making the trip. As he shook my hand, he told me how excited he was to have the opportunity to meet me. I felt honored and special, in a way that made me take a step back, and appreciate just how lucky I was to be a part of this moment. His confidence was impenetrable but tempered by his humble charm. He commanded attention and respect, yet gave it right back to each and every one of us in the room.

With the vigor of a game day locker room speech, Neuheisel hyped up the room by talking up the University of Colorado football program and assured us that we were in for a special weekend. A weekend like no other program could put on. This would be the best recruiting trip we'd ever experience, "So enjoy!"

As soon as Neuheisel said, "enjoy," a bevy of waiters entered the room in choreographed fashion serving plates for the recruits who just entered the room. I was witnessing waiters bringing out some of the largest portions I had ever seen. Of course I had to go with one of those expensive steaks on the menu. It was amazingly tender; I mean a toddler with no molars, or even an old person with dentures could have devoured it. I had no idea that a steak could melt in your mouth like that.

As our late lunch came to a close, we all left to return to the Dal Ward Athletic Center. Once back, coach Neuheisel instructed all of the recruits to go downstairs to the equipment room and pick up a jacket. Nobody thought twice about it as we did what we were told. Our curiosity certainly peaked once jackets were on and a chartered bus pulled up to the Dal Ward steps. Then coach Neuheisel announced that we were going to spend the day on the slopes. WE WERE GOING SKIING! "Wow!" I thought, "This coach is fun as hell."

Colorado is world renowned for its mountains and ski slopes, and the 45-minute trip was well worth the wait. The recruits poured off the bus and onto the scene where we were met by a good majority of the C.U. Buffaloes' current players. I was astonished that the team was skiing. After all, they still had yet to play against Washington in the Holiday Bowl. If any of the players were injured on the slopes, the media would eat Neuheisel alive for allowing his players to do the unthinkable. Clearly, Neuheisel could care less what others thought. He marched to the beat of his own drum and it was obvious that his players loved this about him.

It was on the slopes that I came to know Rashidi Barnes and Marcus Stiggers. Both players were true freshman on the team at the time; however, both were already receiving a little playing time. Marcus was a fast, fleet-footed receiver out of Dallas, Texas. Rashidi was an athletic free safety out of Berkeley, California. This was not the first time I had encountered Rashidi.

I quickly recalled my sophomore year when our high schools played against each other. C.U. had wisely orchestrated it, so that each recruit would be hosted by a group of players at all times. They made sure that the group selected to entertain you, were players who shared either the same position as you, shared your hometown, or had something in common. Marcus and Rashidi were trying to do their best sales pitch to get me on the slopes with them.

It had been a while since I had been skiing, but that's not what had me concerned about the slopes. It was the "mono-ski" that worried me. They were snowboarding, and my first reaction was, "HELL NO!" I was a city boy and there is no way in the world anyone was getting Terrence Wood on a snowboard. But a good thirty minutes later, I found myself receiving a crash course on how to snowboard for the first time. The female instructor was rather attractive, so she kept my attention until she explained how primitive the breaking system was. She instructed, "When the snowboard begins to pick up too much speed, just fall backwards." That just sounded like a recipe for disaster to me.

But Marcus and Rashidi managed to peer pressure me enough that I found myself riding a ski lift with a snowboard attached to the bottom of my snow boots. The lift dumped us off at the top of a huge mountain. This was no place for a beginner. I was fully prepared to sit at the top of that mountain all day if it meant that I didn't have to risk my life snowboarding back down. My better judgment was once again trumped by the daring duo compelling me to go against my better judgment and fears.

There I was, headed down the steepest mountain I had ever been on in my life. I didn't have ski poles to bob and weave through the traffic of trees and rocks like I was accustomed to. I began to get scared as the wide base of the snowboard began to quickly pick up speed. I felt like a torpedo out of control. As I headed down the mountain I knew I needed to stop! Falling backwards to stop seemed like the most illogical maneuver to regain control. It didn't seem like I'd make it past day one of this recruiting adventure.

As cliché as it may sound, life as I knew it was flashing by in fast-forward. And in my despaired state, I made a spur-of-the-moment decision that ultimately saved my life. I doubt that even two seconds had elapsed, but the decision was somehow clear as I finally did what the instructor said. I threw myself backwards into the snow. Unfortunately, I put my arm back first and it buckled right behind my snowboard. A sharp pain shot up my arm and I was sure that I had broken my arm. Miraculously, God had spared me. I was fine. This, I decided, would be the first and last time I'd ever snowboard. From the safety of the bottom of the slopes, I found a seat and watched everyone else take on the beastly slopes for the rest of the day.

Four hours had passed and the first bus was ready to head back to Boulder. I was the first one in line. I couldn't wait to get out of those cold, wet, clothes and return to the comfort and warmth of my hotel room to take a shower. We stayed at the Millennium hotel down the street from the team's football stadium. It was a huge hotel and just like when I visited the University of Virginia, it was elaborately adorned with Buffalo regalia: everything from official uniforms to photographs of celebratory wins.

I checked into my room, glad to see I didn't have a roommate, and hit the recruit lounge that was set up in one of the hotel meeting rooms. Everyone in the room was a BIG TIME recruit and each one had the luxury of not only considering Colorado, but a host of other National Championship contending schools. The room was full of large egos. Each player sized up the other while gathering and exchanging information on the various college ball opportunities. Here, was more "game" being spoken than being played. You could quickly tell that everyone was ultra competitive. Even within a subtle setting, athletes were asking each other probing questions to try and gauge a competitor's football skill or football worth.

I took an immediate liking to a big offensive lineman out of Federal Way, Washington, by the name of Victor Rogers. "Big Vic" was as cool as a fan. Small, fast guys like myself, usually never kick it with the big guys in the trenches, but Vic was different. He didn't seem wrapped up in the whole "sizing each other up" routine. Vic just wanted to have a good time with someone likeminded. I was considered one of the top players available in Northern California, but after a little bit of dialogue with Vic, it became pretty obvious to me that he was the biggest thing to come out of the entire state of Washington. Vic had scholarship offers from just about every school in the country. Vic was a unanimous first team All-American selection by *Prep Star, Student Sports, Super Prep,* and *USA Today. Prep Football Report* classified Vic as the #1 offensive linemen in the country, and the #38 prospect overall. So for a lack of better words, Vic was the bomb!

An hour had passed in the game room and we found ourselves deep in conversation when a few Colorado football players came into the game room to round us up for a night out on college row. Big Vic and I decided to stick together. We hopped in the car excited to see what the night would bring our way. Just like in Virginia, our first stop was the liquor store. I thought to myself, " I guess this is what it's like to be a student athlete regardless of what school you go to."

The liquor was purchased, brown bagged, then consumed on our way to the party. Vic and I consumed drink for drink with everyone in the car. Looking over at our driver, I realized it was the first time in my life I had ever seen someone take shots of rum, or any kind of liquor, and literally drive at the same time. I won't reveal the driver's name, because I'm not here to rat anyone out, but I will say that he was a first team all Big XII player in some publications, and did get drafted. So of course, as an impressionable high school kid, I was going to drink ounce for ounce with him.

I found it somewhat surreal that I was actually partying with the guys that I watched on television every Saturday. By the time we got to the party, I was drunk. It wasn't a babysitting type of drunk, but I was definitely "tipsy"—and for a cold winter night in Colorado, I sure felt warm inside. The women at the party got my mind off of the cold weather as well. It seemed as if everyone was having a ball—people were laughing, drinking, smoking weed, and having one hell of a time. Vic and I were already drunk, so the party was fully endorsed by us. And once again, it didn't seem as if anyone was concerned about possible consequences. It was the culture, and Vic and I were fully engaged.

I did have an incredible time that night. The atmosphere was fun, the guys on the team were cool and I really enjoyed coach Neuheisel and the coaching staff. Neuheisel kept his recruits busy on their visits and he went with a hard-sell approach. I don't blame him, given that he only had a 48-hour window to convert a recruit into a believer in the C.U. program, the university, and the campus life. I went to bed that night in a lavish hotel room, visualizing myself wearing the black and gold of the Colorado Buffaloes.

After breakfast the next day, coach Embree picked my mother and me up for an academic meeting at Dal Ward. There we met up with four other recruits and were put in the care of a special welcome committee that would serve as our official tour guides. On our express tour of the campus, we met the head of the journalism department, which was my major of choice.

Oh, by the way! Did I tell you that our welcome committee wasn't comprised of your average, boring, nerdy tour guides? Our tour guides were four lovely young ladies from the dance team. This amazingly fine woman named Dee blew me away. I found myself wondering, "How were we supposed to focus on academics while being escorted by girls from the *dance squad*?"

The girls led us to the academic orientation held in one of the smaller classrooms on campus. The recruits, the head of the journalism department, our dance team hosts, and some of the recruit parents were all in attendance. During the whole academic presentation I was slouched down in my seat trying to get in quick looks at Dee without my mom noticing. I remember getting more and more pumped up about getting out of my parents house with every single glance I took at Dee. To this day, I'm rather clueless about the information presented in that orientation. At that time, I was motivated purely by libido and ego.

Later that day I finally got the chance to rap with Dee. I told her that I planned on getting back in contact with her as soon as I returned to C.U. She asked if I had decided to attend the university, and I told her that I had not officially elected to do so, but she was certainly making it hard for me to decline the opportunity. We finished the conversation with her blushing and walking away. I was young and cocky, as were all the other recruits on the trip. I had quickly learned along my athletic journey as a young man that football players were catered to by the fans, and especially by the girls. Women were one of the perks that came with the sport as early as I could remember. It's an entertainer's life.

The next stop on our trip was the official tour of the Dal Ward Athletic Center. We started at the top and worked our way downstairs. First, we toured where the scholarship athletes had their meals, which they called the "training table". Then we surveyed the study hall rooms, which had magnificent views of the football stadium. These were prime areas to watch a game. Next we visited the academic advisor offices, which also housed the computer lab. This was the first time I got to meet Erin Hoage, who had the daunting task of making sure everyone on the Colorado football team stayed academically eligible to compete every fall weekend.

After that, it was time to go down to the main entrance level to view the rest of the facility. The first stop on this level was the athletic training rooms. As you walked through the double doors it felt as if you had entered sacred ground. It was the place where trainers and doctor's taped players, revived injured players, and made big medical decisions that could easily hinder or aid a player's career. The area was enormous. There were doctors' offices, X-Ray machines, muscle stem machines, and a training pool to assist in rehabbing, treadmills, stair masters, and bicycles. It was definitely a big-time training facility, but it was also a place that no athlete would want to spend much time in.

The training room was also connected to the team's very impressive weight room facility. I felt like I had walked into the US Olympic training headquarters. There were men and women working their butts off! At the time, Colorado had the best strength coach in the country, named Doctor Kries. "Doc" was named one of the top ten "Master Strength and Conditioning Coaches" by the Collegiate Strength and Conditioning association in 2001. The Professional Football Strength and Conditioning Coaches Association twice named him "National Collegiate Strength Coach of The Year". So the man knows how to get the most out of his athletes! The great thing about Doc Kries was that he didn't care if you were a Heisman Trophy candidate, or if you never touched the field; he pushed everyone equally. He pushed extraneously *hard*! Once we entered "his" weight room, as he put it, all the recruits were Doc's property. You could tell he was passionate about his job because of the amount of enthusiasm and passion his tour offered. Doc had a sincere respect and love for all of "his" athletes at the University of Colorado. The weight room was beautiful. There were C.U. emblems everywhere you looked, even on the weights, and the entire weight room overlooked the football stadium, and served as a fantastic viewing area. I met up with the rest of the group and caught the very end of the stadium tour. The stadium was beautiful, and all I could imagine was running out to thousands of screaming fans right behind "Ralphie, the Buffalo," the best mascot in college football.

After the tour we headed out to lunch with a couple of players at the local mall. It was cool to get a feel for the town and not just the school. Remember, when you are making a decision on where to attend college, in most cases you are making a 4-to-5-year-long decision. Every recruit needs to look at as many factors as possible if he wants to make a sound decision. Believe me, getting a good feel for the city, and in some cases the surrounding cities of the university, can definitely be helpful. It's important to evaluate what is important to you. If your hometown is a big city, then you might feel stifled at a small-town university. Carefully weigh your surroundings and the offer being presented to you.

All of us recruits were looking forward to the team's "Big Bowl Game Party" later that evening. The team had finished third in the Big XII in 1996 and had been invited to play against the Washington Huskies in the Holiday Bowl. The C.U. football team had rented out a local nightclub in order to celebrate their tremendous year of play. The only people invited to the party were the coaches, current players, recruits, and beautiful women! No parents or outsiders were permitted. However, Neuheisel had scheduled a nice dinner at the Dal Ward Athletic Center for the recruits and their families before the party. I must commend the football program for really rolling out the red carpet for that dinner in particular. Everything was catered and the food was fabulous. There were black and gold linens on the tables, football helmets and jerseys strategically placed throughout the room. The backdrop was the phenomenal nighttime view of the stadium that we all had from our seats.

After everyone had been seated and plates were served, the lights began to dim. A large projection screen dropped down from the ceiling and began highlight clips, to music, for each recruit in the room. This was well thought out and very personalized. It was cool to get a good look at what the other recruits in the room had to offer. It was at this moment when it hit me that I was truly good enough to play Big Time College Football. I casually noticed coach Neuheisel going in and out of the room every fifteen minutes, pulling players out one by one. I really didn't read too much into it until I saw my new friend, "Big Vic," get tapped on the shoulder by Neuheisel. I took special interest in his absence. About 20 minutes had passed and Big Vic had yet to return to his seat. An assistant coach informed me that Neuheisel requested for me to head back to his office.

To my surprise, I found Big Vic was still in the office. Coach Neuheisel instructed me to sit down on the couch next to Vic. Coach sat on the edge of his big oak desk with his guitar in hand. I thought to myself, "I knew this guy was the head football coach, and I knew he was a licensed lawyer, but damn, he's a musician too?" Neuheisel told me how he wanted both Victor Rogers and I to play football for the University of Colorado. However, Vic had just informed Coach Neuheisel that he would not commit to the University of Colorado unless I committed as well!

Neuheisel proceeded to ask, "So what do we have to do to make this happen?" I looked at Coach Neuheisel long and hard, then glanced back at Vic, who had the biggest "I-got-you" smile, I had ever seen on somebody's face before. As I took a minute to contemplate my fate, I looked out Coach Neuheisel's window onto Folsom Field. Something about that moment just felt right. So right then and there in Neuheisel's office, Victor Rogers and I gave verbal commitments to become Buffaloes! Neuheisel walked us back to the dinner table with a happy salesman's grin on his face. Two more top recruits bagged, and a full room to go.

Vic and I were already making big plans for our careers in black and gold, as we walked back to the dining area. We had the perfect place to celebrate our decision later on that evening. The recruit party was about to be out of control. My mother observed the big smile on my face as we entered the room and made our way back to our seats, but I don't think it ever crossed her mind that I would commit without talking to her or my father first. I knew that it would be best for me to keep it a secret for as long as possible in order to not ruffle either of my parent's feathers. Mum was the word.

To my surprise, the news had already been leaked to the C.U. coaching staff. It was time to head to the party and some of the guys on the team came by the hotel to get us drunk before we headed out. Once they heard Vic and I committed, it seemed as if the high fives and drinks came faster than ever. Once again, my judgment turned to putty when confronted with the college way of life. I was already getting "turned out" and I hadn't even attended a single day of school yet. Needless to say, it wouldn't be appropriate for me to talk about what happened the rest of the night. But I will confirm, it was the time of my life!

The next morning was our exit day. Neuheisel scheduled an informal meeting over breakfast to have a word with my mother and me. Neuheisel thanked us for coming on the trip and then let my mother know he was officially offering me a scholarship. Then he went on to mention that he heard I was the talk of the town at the team party. My mother gave me one of those, "What in the hell did you do?" looks. I put my head down and smiled at my plate. My mother thanked coach Neuheisel and let him know that we would like to discuss the offer as a family, then get back to him with our final decision. I said goodbye to "Big Vic" for now, and my mother and me headed to the airport.

Our flight departed on time and I already began to feel homesick for a place I had just barely become familiar with. I stared out the aircraft window, wishing I didn't have to go. I had just finished my second recruiting trip and between coach Neuheisel, Big Vic and the beautiful ladies, Colorado was looking highly favorable in my mind. But as I said before, in the recruiting game, things have a way of changing every day!

CHAPTER 5

The Sales Pitch

MOST PEOPLE DO not group college coaches and salesmen together. But many college coaches are better than any salesmen, in any field you will ever come across! The "sales pitch" is the most important tool in a college coach's toolbox. It's interesting that many of them don't get more credit for their sales acumen. It takes something special to consistently attract the TOP talent in the country to your school, year after year. The best recruiters do a great job of not only selling the school, but also selling themselves. They sell themselves, and their coaching staff, as the group who is best suited to take a prospect to the next level. I would assume it gets hard to manage 85 scholarship and non-scholarship team members, while simultaneously making television appearances, attending alumni events, and most importantly—winning games. Some of the things these coaches will say and do in order to attract talent are legendary. Promises are part of the rules of engagement when trying to nab the best prospects before a rival school does.

Remember, this is a competitive battlefield among top football programs across the country. Coaches have to be able to hustle, "spit game," and outsmart their opponents long before they see them on the football field. Prosperity is the reward for any BUSINESS that is soundly planned and executed.

Coaches are artists when it comes to wooing highly recruited prospects. They want to make sure that the offer will cater to that player's needs. The only way to guarantee a favorable outcome is to ask recruits open-ended questions, such as, "What will it take to get you to be a part of our program?" I'm sure you can imagine some of the wild responses coaches have heard from recruits and their family after asking a question like that. I noted first hand the highly touted negotiating magic of Rick Neuheisel. Not only was he good at getting the players that he wanted, but he was also good at identifying who was the actual decision maker was in the prospect's family.

Known by many as "Slick Rick" for his charisma and aptitude for sliding past the rules, he was careful not to break them, or should I say not breaking the big ones! Coach Neuheisel had a reputation for going into California and Texas and plucking out their most heralded recruits. Although historically this had been nearly impossible to do, he seemed to make it look easy. I believe what made this magic possible was his confidence, sincerity, and ability to win the trust of the athletes and their parents, or guardians. People do business with people they like. Rick Neuheisel is a master at getting you to like him! In addition, his proven track record of winning during his two years at C.U. made his word as solid as oak. While in pursuit of my talent, Coach Neuheisel was coming off of two 10-win seasons in only his first two years of handling the head coaching duties at the University of Colorado.

Neuheisel truly had the golden touch and was a very hot commodity: he was the youngest head coach in D1-A football and had been rumored every day to be heading to the NFL to fill one of few vacant head coaching jobs there. This debate of whether or not he would go to the NFL created doubt in the minds of my parents. What good is it to "gift wrap" your child and send him off to a university if the head coach doesn't even plan on staying there himself?

If at all possible, you'll want to play your whole career under the guidance of the same head coach who recruits you. Your success in football is never guaranteed. But when playing under the hand of a head coach who believed his school should recruit you in the first place, the odds of getting a good opportunity to succeed are definitely better than playing for a coach who has no loyalty to you.

Football, like any other business, is based on supply and demand. The team is in the business of providing entertainment, and in order to give the demanding crowd a great show for their buck, they must bring in the most entertaining performers.

Scholarships afford universities the opportunity to expand the talent pool and deliver unforgettable football season performances through diversity outreach. Let's face it, the odds of a kid from the hood of south Florida having the opportunity to attend a school like Duke based on academic achievement alone are rather unlikely, but not completely implausible. It also gives a budding athlete an opportunity to be exposed to other worlds that he may not otherwise have the chance to explore. Sport-based scholarships are, in essence, a payout to attract an unlikely candidate to seriously consider a school outside of his typical realm of possibility. But they are not handed out like bubble gum. It takes a special candidate and a believing coach to make this "marriage" between school and student athlete a reality.

A courtship of this kind often culminates with an in home visit from a recruiter/coach for a little one-on-one Q & A session with the prospects family. It's college football's version of sending in the closer for the sale. I can still remember the day that "Slick Rick" came to my family's house, like it was yesterday. At that time our family actually had one of those universal weight room sets in our garage. I was there, curling weights and circuit training in an attempt to make my little high school muscles pop out. My dad was upstairs trying to prepare all of the fatherly questions he could come up with, and my mom was getting some snacks and drinks ready to welcome coach Neuheisel and coach Embree (The Bay Area recruiter for the C.U. football program).

Once the doorbell rang, we all rushed into our places to get ready for our meeting. I was still in shock that the hottest coach in college football at the time was literally in my house. My parents were equally excited for this moment, but we all did our best to stay levelheaded and not let ourselves become distracted by the glory.

The night was going great and coach Neuheisel was knocking down every question my dad was shooting at him. But there was one question my dad was saving for the right time. Finally, he pulled it out. My father looked coach Neuheisel in his eyes, congratulated him on all his success and then said, "I can't help but hear your name connected with all of the NFL head coach vacancies. How long do you seriously plan on staying at Colorado?"

With a straight and sincere face, Neuheisel replied, "I promise you, Mr. and Mrs. Wood, that I will be at the University of Colorado the entire duration of Terrence's career!"

Little did I know, at the time, the effect on my future, or the impact of the coach's statement would be so significant. People fail to realize the domino effect caused by the shuffling around of a coaching staff. It is essential to remember that Big Time College Football is a business and a coach's word is only as strong as his next big contract, or strategic opportunity. Money talks and many are left behind as a mere casualty of the game. My family and I decided to focus on the University of Colorado as a highly probable reality for me. We put a lot of trust in the guidance and direction of coach Neuheisel. It felt right! Neuheisel made me a believer in the university, and more importantly, in him as a coach. I don't know if it was the look in his eyes or the conviction in his voice, but I could tell that he was on the verge of creating something special at CU, and I desperately wanted to be a part of it. I was sold!

CHAPTER 6

Decision Time

ONE OF THE most rewarding, yet stressful times, in a young athlete's life is the decision about where to go to school. Many recruits feel pulled in different directions by the opinions of the people around them, many find themselves struggling to find people they can really confide in. One thing that is very important to remember is that everyone will carry an opinion about what should be done. But opinions are like mouths, everyone has one. If you live your life based on opinion, then you will find yourself constantly lost, searching for truth and hopping from one idea to the next based on someone's view of the world. This is no way to secure a future. When you are trying to become a pro athlete you cannot afford to be a ping-pong ball, jumping from one side of the fence to the other. Again, I stress that it is essential that a prospect have a very tight knit center of influence, a group of people who can help filter out all the information needed to make a sound decision.

With increased high school exposure, press conferences are now commonplace for high-profile high school players when announcing their college of choice. This can place even more pressure on a kid because now the whole world is watching. Keep in mind that this is your decision. No one else is going to live in the dorms for you, go to class for you, or go through training camp for you. So why in the hell should they be the sole-decision maker for you? Listen to the people you trust and then decide for yourself.

Take Julio Jones for instance. Now the star receiver for the Atlanta Falcons, Julio was considered the #1 Wide Receiver in all the 2008 football-recruiting publications. As crazy as it sounds, Julio was quoted saying he was "relieved to get the recruiting process over, when he was in high school." He expressed that it was a breath of fresh air not to have to receive any more phone calls from college coaches and the media. The pressure of being named "Mr. Football" in the state of Alabama, along with ample media coverage was more than many fringe NFL players ever receive. Jones recalled during his signing day interview that when the recruiting process began it was great, but people took it a little too far. It had gotten to the point where he had to wear a hooded sweatshirt in many public places so that he could go on with some sense of normalcy.

Although there was no press conference to announce my college decision, I definitely felt the pressure. The level of pressure I experienced from the schools recruiting me increased dramatically upon returning home from my recruiting trips. I guess the schools figure after they wine and dine you they deserve an answer from you. I was already leaning towards the University of Colorado, but I must admit, it was the great sales tactics of Rick Neuheisel that finalized the deal.

One of the greatest tactics a salesman could ever use on a prospective client or customer is "the fear of loss". Fear is a great motivator, and has long been used to control the masses. If you fear that a great offer will be taken off the table, you will be reactionary in your decision-making instead of being proactive and in control.

When Neuheisel asked me one day about my decision, over the phone, I told coach Neuheisel I wanted to take my time with my decision, and possibly take another recruiting trip, he used that "fear of loss" tactic on me! He told me, "Terrence, I definitely understand that you want to take your time with your decision and make no mistake about it, I definitely want you to be a part of our team. But I'm only signing two corners in this year's recruiting class. I can't hold onto these scholarships for long, our program is very attractive right now. If someone at your position commits to us first, we may not have a scholarship still available for you."

Neuheisel could tell I was on the fence about my decision so he had to put the squeeze on me, and it certainly worked! Neuheisel was determined to make me a Buffalo, not only for the fact that I was a pretty damn good player, but also because "Big Vic" had already told him that we were a package deal. With my commitment, Neuheisel knew he would have the #1 offensive lineman in the country bagged as well. When you can get two prospects during the courting of just one, it's always considered time well spent and an investment well earned. Top recruits equal top teams, which equals top dollar for college coaches, and Rick Neuheisel was well on his way to adding more cushion to his bank account with the recruiting class of 1997.

Needless to say, **I officially committed to the University of Colorado the next day!** There was NO way in the world I was going to lose out on that scholarship and let another corner commit.

CHAPTER 7

My First Contract

WHEN YOU REALLY break down how much money goes into a kid getting a full-ride scholarship, we're easily talking about a six-figure investment that some of these schools are making towards each potential recruit. For example, when the University of Virginia offered me a full-ride scholarship as an out-of-state student, they were basically telling my parents that they were willing to subsidize me roughly $30,000 a year to play football for their program. Currently, the out of state tuition for the University of Virginia is about $40,000 a year. To put it in perspective, the United States Department of Commerce provided a statistic stating that the average income for Americans age 25 or older was roughly $38,000, when I came out of high school. So when a school offers a scholarship, they are offering REAL MONEY! The level of education and the opportunities that college will provide for your future are life changing. The college degree is a goal that is available for you to take advantage of, if you <u>choose</u> to. Those who are wise will diversify their investment and take full advantage of the scholarship from both an athletic and educational standpoint.

Now, the reason young ball players need to really grasp the correlation between a scholarship and a contract is for the business implications behind the two. For many athletes, a scholarship is the first time they will sign their name on a document that involves serious money. But tied to that scholarship is an obligation that you must fulfill with the university and its athletic department. You now represent the school as a student and as an athlete. You have been *blessed* with the opportunity to let your God-given talents provide the means for your education. Wow!

Unfortunately, too many players have it backwards. They think college is the means to exposure and success as an athlete. Remember: the number of athletes who fail to play in the NFL will always outweigh the number of those who succeed. More players fall in the trenches and trappings of getting to the big time, with no backup plan or degree to fall back on. It behooves you to avoid becoming a statistic by having your education be your foundation. That way, regardless of whether you *go pro* or not, you will have a means to provide for yourself and your family.

You have to remember, with big blessings come big expectations and responsibilities. Basically, when that football coach says jump, you ask, "HOW HIGH?" When that strength coach says run, you fly! And when that academic advisor demands summer school, you go. You uphold your end of the contract or risk losing it all and being sent home! The moment someone pays for you to play, whether it's a scholarship or an NFL contract, your mentality has to switch to that of a business mindset.

Many go to college and get sent right back home because they can't uphold their side of the contract. Whether it's grades, or substance abuse issues, you must still fulfill all your commitments. At the collegiate level, everyone is on contract. The coach is on contract, the head doctor is on contract, and the athletic director is on contract. Everybody. In high school, a coach may lose for ten years without winning a league game, and still hold on to his job. But college coaches being fired is always a part of the headlines of every football season. Urban Meyer, the head coach at Ohio State University, would literally fear for his life if he went one season without winning a league game, as passionate as the Ohio State fans are. Many schools will "buy out" a coach's contract just to get rid of him. Just ask the Cal Bears about that. According to the *Daily Californian*, Cal paid coach Jeff Tedford $5.4 million to part ways.

An athlete can really succeed when given the right perspective about his or her situation. It's understood that a college football player must go into professional football with a business mindset. But more importantly, I believe it is essential for high school players to go into college with that same business mindset. When a high school player signs a letter of intent to attend a university, he is signing a full-blown contract. Contracts represent business, and it can be detrimental for a young athlete NOT to look at it that way!

CHAPTER 8

Educated Decisions Are a Must

LET ME START off by saying that any parent or guardian who thinks their kid has what it takes to play college football, must make sure their child is academically eligible to play college football first! Bluntly put, there is no point in pursuing a college athletic scholarship if your kid does not qualify with the NCAA Clearinghouse. Each year there are too many great athletes who never make it to college due to disqualification per NCAA Clearinghouse rules. There *are* minimum requirements that a child must fulfill to become a student athlete at the college level! If you are in high school, ask your school guidance counselor, or check out NCAA.com to get more information on the NCAA Clearinghouse (college football's eligibility authority).

Most college coaches prefer that a prospect be on file with the Clearinghouse even before he plays in his first game in his senior year of high school. If it's not done by the end of your first semester your senior year, there is a good chance you will officially FORFEIT your opportunity to play college football for at least one year. That's the bottom line.

It is essential for parents and guardians of talented athletes to do their due diligence when it comes to ensuring prime opportunities for their most precious assets, their children! The decision on where to attend college will have big implications for the rest of one's life. I personally met my wife, and had my first child in the same city where I went to college. **It's not a decision to be taken lightly, or even solely based on a sport.** It only makes sense that the parents, guardians, and advisors of these young athletes work together to gather as much information as they possibly can, about the potential schools they may be considering.

Teenagers will make naïve decisions based upon how they feel at a particular time. So, the best thing any athlete could have is someone like a parent, guardian, or an advisor, be a filter to assist in the athlete's college decision. There must be someone who can act as the voice of clarity and insight during a time that can be really confusing for a Big Time College Football prospect.

In my opinion, this role model is absent in many student athletes' lives. A lot of families go wrong during the recruiting process because they are ill equipped to navigate through this process. College football recruiting is very similar to the stock market. You talk to a flashy coach, similar to a stockbroker, he blows you away with the possibilities of how your investments can boom if you choose to work with his company. He paints the picture of the end result, which includes a lavish lifestyle, retirement, nice homes and vacations. It's fool proof, right? Never once is there any talk of loss, or sub-par performance by those stocks. So you dive right in with faulty rationale: 80% faith, 10% research, and 10% other people's opinions, just to find out five years down the road that your money has barely doubled, you've overspent, and lived way beyond your means. Now you owe more than you have saved and are probably going to work until you die, just to pay off the debt you've accumulated. To make matters worse, the guy who was originally managing your investments never intended on staying with that company in the first place. So, just like stocks, there are no absolute guarantees when it comes to recruiting. But it doesn't have to be a total crapshoot either!

Warren Buffet, who has been widely considered to be the greatest investor our country has ever seen, once said, "I never jump into anything blindly." But so many times just like that "stockbroker," the flashy college coach comes into your home and makes promises he might not be able to fulfill. And what do we do? We hand over our investment (our children), on faith and opinion instead of thorough research, while anxiously waiting for 3 to 5 years to see if we made the right decision.

Someone who does not know about the process can gain a vast amount of knowledge by seeking out people in the know. Trust me, the investment of your time will be time well spent when you look back upon the recruiting process. PARENTS, I URGE YOU TO DO YOUR DUE DILLIGENCE!

CHAPTER 9

Never Burn Bridges

LEARNING HOW TO preserve relationships will be one of the most valuable lessons for a young athlete who wants to get into Big Time College or Professional Football! All high-level football coaches know each other, and they all move around within their respective ranks. That coach you hung up on from San Jose State could be the offensive coordinator for the New England Patriots by the time its your year to get drafted. And believe me, coaches do not forget players they have had contact with, especially if you burn them! My family has an extensive football background, so I was told never to "burn bridges" early on in my career. And I am sure glad I took advantage of that advice. Looking back, I can remember there being many opportunities for me to "burn bridges" or possibly rub a coach the wrong way.

One example was when San Jose State University had set their sights on recruiting me. Coach Ruben Carter, the former NFL Defensive Lineman for the Broncos, and longtime College and NFL coach, was my contact. San Jose State is a smaller market Division 1A football team, with a history of having terrible seasons when I was in high school. San Jose State would be comparable to Southern Methodist University down south, Wyoming University in the mid-west, and Temple University in the east. They're all great schools, they all have Division 1A Football teams, but they all have a history of fielding losing football teams. To San Jose State's credit, it seems as if their program is getting stronger.

Given that I was receiving attention from top-15-ranked schools, San Jose State was definitely not on my list of schools to visit. I could have easily just shrugged off coach Carter, and not have given him the time of day! But I knew it was not be in the best interest of my long-term career. As a matter of fact, coach Carter and I actually formed a pretty good relationship during my exploration of San Jose State. And although coach Carter ended up getting a job at the University of Maryland right in the middle of trying to recruit me to San Jose State, he continued his pursuit of me. Since he liked me so much, he actually tried to sway me to take a trip to the University of Maryland after he arrived! It was a definite upgrade from San Jose State, but not enough to make me think twice about my decision to go to Colorado. However, I deeply appreciated his gesture. The reality is that the University of Maryland offer could have proved valuable if everything had fallen through with my Colorado scholarship offer.

I've heard plenty of horror stories about guys who had a scholarship revoked from a school so late in the recruiting process that they ended up losing out on all of the other schools they were considering as well.

The lesson of NEVER Burning Bridges has also rung true recently in my life as I have found myself calling old coaches to get some of the young players I mentor opportunities to play at the college and professional level. I have received tickets to games, and invites to NFL workouts from former coaches, for some of my aspiring athletes. There are countless stories of athletes who have received a "thumbs up" or "thumbs down" verdict for a particular roster spot based on their relationship with certain coaches they have come across during their career. It is <u>essential</u> for any athlete who is serious about their football career to exercise this lesson of "never burning bridges" It very well can make or break your career!

CHAPTER 10

Neuheisel's Great Recruiting Class

ONCE THE DUST cleared and the smoke had settled on signing day back in 1997, according to most publications, Neuheisel had managed to pull off the #5 ranked recruiting class in the country. Colorado had managed to get the top two players out of the state of Washington that year, with a big six-foot-three 245-pound linebacker, Tyler Gregorak, and my future roommate, Victor Rogers. "Big Vic" was a mammoth-sized kid, at six-foot-six 315 pounds. Neuheisel then pulled off a double play in Houston TX by signing, arguably, the top two players in the state; Cedric Cormier, a speedy option quarterback, who was going to be converted into a wide receiver, and Andre Gurode, a big physical interior offensive lineman, who is most known for his Pro Bowl years as a center with the Dallas Cowboys.

This was only Neuheisel's second season as the headman at Colorado. He had inherited a physical option team from legendary Colorado coach, Bill McCartney, who had brought the first and only National Championship trophy back to the University of Colorado in 1990. Neuheisel had a very clear objective of what he wanted the identity of his team to be, and that was FAST. Neuheisel made his recruiting reputation off of grabbing some of the best, fastest, and most skilled players in the country. Coach Neuheisel was a true believer in the phrase "speed kills." We could have easily fielded a highly ranked 400-meter relay team with many of the guys we had on our football team. Then, to put the icing on his recruiting cake, Neuheisel pulled in four Defensive backs out of the golden state of

California for the 1997 Colorado Football recruiting class. He certainly held true to his word by only signing two cornerbacks that year, and I was just elated to be one of them.

You could just feel the buzz around the University of Colorado program! There was an overwhelming feeling of optimism that we were ready to take on Nebraska. You see, in the late 1990's, in order to win the BIG XII Conference, you had to go through Nebraska. The University of Colorado had fielded many teams that had National Championship potential. Unfortunately, the team that ended up knocking them off each year happened to be within the same conference. Lincoln, Nebraska is the home to four National Championship trophies and has always been a thorn in the tail of the Buffaloes: The 1994 Colorado Buffaloes had a Heisman Trophy winner, a Thorpe award winner, a future Butkus award winner, and plenty of award finalists on their team. The 1994 Buffaloes also had a record of 11-1, finishing their season off with a complete massacre of the Notre Dame Fighting Irish in the Fiesta Bowl. The only problem with that '94 Colorado Buffaloes team was the fact that the team who went 12-0 that year and won the National Championship was, Nebraska.

The Nebraska Cornhuskers had a reputation of being a physical team who would literally manhandle the schools they played against. Neuheisel figured that the key to beating coach Tom Osborne's Nebraska Cornhuskers would be to use superior speed. Neuheisel wanted to develop a menacing, swarming defense, and an explosive, high scoring offense. Much like the blueprints that teams like Florida and USC have used to bring their programs to national prominence, Neuheisel was fully aware that in order to bring another National Championship Trophy back to Boulder, we could not play Nebraska's game. Instead, we would make Nebraska play *our* game. And in order for Nebraska to play our game, they were going to have to SPEED UP!

CHAPTER 11

Welcome To College

THERE IS NO way I could possibly find the words to express how excited I was to go off to college. When I was younger, I never imagined I would end up at Colorado, but I was sure glad I did. All of the years I spent cutting out pictures of college football players and watching games every Saturday were officially over. Now the roles were reversed and there would be young kids idolizing *my* plays on Saturdays, and looking up to me. I still get goose bumps thinking back to that time in my life. There is nothing like the feeling you have when your **dreams are realized!**

My father was very excited, and deep down, my mother was too. But there was another side of my mother that was an emotional wreck! Every mom gets that "my baby is growing up" feeling of loss. Most mothers wish that their babies never have to leave, but it's just a part of the evolution of that relationship. The day I was scheduled to get on the plane and leave for college was a day I will never forget. My mother, my aunt, my younger brother, and my high school girlfriend, all piled up in the car for what would be the most emotional ride to the airport I would ever have. All the women's eyes turned into fountains as we pulled out of the driveway. There was very little said, and the silence was stifling. By the time we got to the airport we had become the amusement of other travelers.

Other people in the airport were looking at my family with that, "what in the hell happened to them?" look. We hugged and kissed as long as we possibly could and then I was off! Off to embark upon a new chapter in my life that only God had read the pages to. I never knew it was possible to feel so overwhelmingly sad and excited at the same time. I had a two-hour flight before I reached my destination, and that whole two hours I spent reminiscing on all of the childhood events that got me to this moment in my life. I was leaving California and going to Colorado on a very specific mission, and truthfully, it was NOT to graduate from college. IT WAS TO GO TO THE NFL!

I would guess that at least 80% of the recruits who end up signing with major division 1A football teams feel the same way. It's understandable how athletes put so much focus on their athletic success, but remember: it's never good to put all your eggs in one basket.

My father actually promised me that if I was projected to be at least a second round draft choice at the end of my junior year, I would have his blessing to forgo my senior season and enter the NFL draft instead. And that's exactly what I intended on doing!

Once I arrived on campus I noticed the weather was unexpectedly hot. Colorado is one of those states that can get ice cold in the winter, and blistering hot in the summer. Given that the campus is at an altitude of over 6,000 feet, it sometimes feels like the sun is beating down directly on top of you. I was at home in San Francisco training all summer where the weather never went a degree over 83. So to arrive in Boulder, for my first day of freshman camp, and have to practice in 93-degree weather, it was challenging to say the least. We had two days of freshman camp to give the Coaches an early peak at their NEW toys before the veteran players reported to camp.

Freshman camps are big at every school across the country; it gives everyone a glimpse into the future. The fans, coaches, and media all intensely watched to see if our freshman class was as good as the hype! Even veteran players who arrived early to training camp came by to get a quick peek at the class of 1997. I must say we didn't disappoint. I got plenty of advice from my father and my grandfather on how to standout during big-time competition. The consensus was that I needed to get out of the gates early if I wanted to get playing time as a true freshman. Here's a tip for those who play defense and are trying to make a football team:

expect shorter routes from the receivers early in training camp! Everyone knows that offenses across the country work on their timing early in training camp. It's very important that everyone on the offensive side of the ball is on the same page. So while our offense was busy working on all of their most basic plays, I was busy picking off passes and turning heads.

The best thing you can do when faced with a highly competitive situation is to concentrate on yourself! As cold as it sounds, worrying about others during competition will have you on the bench in college football and without a job in the NFL. I don't care if it happens to be your roommate! Wish everyone the best, but when the day is said and done, make sure you are still one of the last men standing. Since I was a scholarship athlete, I was not fighting for money in my pocket like the guys fighting for an NFL roster spot. I was fighting for RESPECT and a spot on our active college roster. I desperately did not want to red-shirt because I thought "red shirting" was beneath me.

It is a known fact that scholarship athletes who come from high school, as opposed to junior colleges, typically red-shirt. A school has the right to sit out a freshman during his first year to make sure he is ready both mentally and physically to compete at the college level. The following year, the player will be a red-shirt freshman, and still maintain four years of playing eligibility, but has a year of the program under his belt. Red shirting can be beneficial to a player especially if he needs to get bigger, faster, or happens to have a superstar player in front of him on the depth chart. This is a great way to sit the year out, strengthen your game, concentrate on school, and not waste a year on the bench.

As for my plans, red shirting was not an option. I had dreams of the fairytale college career, which involved playing as a true freshman. I was determined to fulfill a three-year athletic college plan. I wanted to walk right on campus and make plays as a freshman, solidify my name as a sophomore, and dominate as a junior. Then make it to "the show", and make money!

Like so many other college players, I looked at the university as a stepping-stone to get to where I really wanted to be, the NFL. Everyone who dreams of one day playing in the NFL knows they must attract the

NFL's attention with what they do in college first. After solidifying myself as a definite player to watch during freshman camp, it was time to practice with the big boys.

The first day of practice with the veterans was a totally different scene compared to our freshman practice. I couldn't really sleep the night before, I was too busy thinking about how I'd fare practicing against the vets when the sun came up. I was going from high school football—where no one was over 18 years old—to Big Time College Football where we actually had a guy who was 26 on our team. As I looked around at some of the guys during practice, I thought to myself, "I'm about to practice against some grown men!" A couple of my new teammates looked old enough to be my dad. I quickly realized then and there, that I was no longer the "big man on campus." We had a bunch of guys ranked for numerous preseason college football awards, as well as guys who were forecasted to make big money in the NFL soon. I was just a freshman who needed to find a way to catch everyone's attention as fast as I possibly could.

As a new freshman joining the team, you realistically have about two weeks to show you're worthy of grabbing early playing time. Most coaches have a pretty good idea early on of potential contributors. But after the first two weeks of training camp, coaches must turn their attention to the first game's opponent. There is no time to waste, every second counts when trying to make an impression in training camp!

Suited up and ready to practice, I froze in awe of my new playing environment. There were more fans watching my first college practice than at any of the high school games that I had ever played in. News cameramen, reporters, NFL scouts, and devoted fans all make up the audience. This was commonplace at Big Time Football programs.

As I ran out onto the practice field, I could actually hear fans and reporters saying, "good luck, Terrence!" and, "We're glad you chose Colorado!" I was baffled. How did these people know my name?

Anyone that has ever accomplished anything BIG in life has had to carry themselves with a certain level of confidence just to survive, let alone succeed. If you don't believe in yourself, how can you expect anyone else to believe in you? Everywhere around me I saw talented athletes... guys who were capable of making amazing plays at anytime. For my corner-back position alone we had about five guys in front of me that were all great players. Someone without a high level of personal confidence would have tucked in their tale and headed back home. But that was never an option for me. We were the #1 ranked preseason team in the country, according to the *Sporting News Magazine*, and even though I was only a true freshman, my goal was to be a major contributor. Unfortunately, Rick Neuheisel had other plans for me, as well as the rest of our recruiting class.

CHAPTER 12

"Cell Block '97"

THE ONLY WAY that a major college football coach can go on the recruiting trail and produce a top-five recruiting class is to go after the best prospects in the country, and promise them all an opportunity to compete. Let me further clarify the difficulty of this feat. A coach must not only promise an athlete the chance to compete, he must also offer the lure of competing as a freshman. As much as I'd love to tell you that everything that comes out of a coach's mouth is as advertised, the reality is, it isn't so. You should also know that things do not always turn out the way we think they should. Most of the kids in my recruiting class were told to expect the opportunity to see early playing time. Unfortunately, it became evident early in training camp that coach Neuheisel had other plans for our recruiting class. Coach Neuheisel was going into his third year as the football leader at the University of Colorado. This means that the class of 1997 was only the second recruiting class in the mold of what coach Neuheisel wanted his team to look like. This brings up an important issue in your decision to go with one college over another. With new staff, comes new vision. A coaching change, whether in college or the pros, is a volatile time for the organization.

Neuheisel was very proud of the 1997 recruiting class, and he was also aware of the fact that he already had a very talented team, with very high expectations. So what he did was make an executive decision to redshirt our entire recruiting class! Out of the 23 players that signed letters of intent to play football for C.U. in 1997, only one of us would see the field that year. That would be Tyler Gregorak, the big linebacker out of the state of Washington.

I believe that if the Buffaloes did not have a pressing need in the linebacker position, Gregorak would have never played our freshman year either. Although Neuheisel's decision did not receive the popular vote of the freshman recruits, the angry fans, or the staff that supported him, he probably assumed it would *benefit* us as a class and him as a coach in the long run if he could keep us all together. The backlash of Neuheisel's decision was an unhealthy balance of complacency among the older guys on the team, and anger from the disgruntled young players. Typically, when someone doesn't have to compete to keep his position in football or any other profession, he stops striving to become better. So our veteran players became stagnant and we never really lived up to the #1 ranking the *Sporting News* gave us. Neuheisel's plan and vision backfired, to say the least.

Understandably, many of the guys in the 1997 recruiting class were eager to transfer before the season even kicked off, because they felt deceived. It was a shame to only have one player touch the field. It would have been acceptable if the decision to red-shirt all of us was based on talent or sub-par performance during training camp, but this was based purely on one man's vision. I felt perplexed. It just didn't make sense! The freshman class was livid and decided that it was time to meet with coach Neuheisel to express our displeasure.

Surprisingly, he recognized, and actually appreciated our competitiveness and intensity. He assured us that his decision to red-shirt everyone was with a greater purpose in mind, but this went in one ear and out the other. We wanted change, and we wanted it NOW! But whether we liked it or not, only one of us would see any real college action until the following year.

As freshmen on the team, our role was to prepare the veteran guys each week to compete in the Big XII. The '97 class collectively developed a major chip on our shoulders. This wasn't necessarily a bad thing. We grew stronger as a class and basically became one. We banded together as brothers and took on the name and the identity of "cell block '97." We felt as though our entire class had been held back and locked down like prisoners against our will. As a class, that year, we pushed each other and supported each other in anticipation of taking over the college football world after our red-shirt sentence was over.

The class of 1997 was hungry to touch the field, and didn't give a damn who or what was in the way. We were determined to bring the first championship back to the University of Colorado. But for now, we had to wait!

CHAPTER 13

Opening Day

THE FIRST GAME of my true freshman year at the University of Colorado was by far the most thrilling event of my 18 years of life. Yes, receiving various scholarship offers was great. Yes, signing my letter of intent meant the world to me. There was even a certain chill that ran down my spine, running out for my first college practice. But none of these events even came close in comparison with the feeling of running out onto the field for my first college football game experience. Even with the freshman class being red-shirted, the experience was stellar.

There was an unbelievable buzz on campus to see what Rick Neuheisel's Buffaloes had in store for the '97 season. Our first game was against our cross-town rival Colorado State—which helped to provide even more hype for our first contest. It's one of the greatest and most heated rivalries in college football. In the state of Colorado, it's everything! Colorado State was well aware of our preseason promise to conquer it all, and they desperately wanted to come into the University of Colorado home stadium and provide an early disappointment to our favorable season.

Our team would stay at the same hotel, the night before every home game. The following day, we mounted our team buses curbside. As our buses pulled off, four police motorcycles rolled up alongside us. I leaned over to Damen Wheeler, one of the starting cornerbacks, and said, "Hey man, I think we're getting pulled over." He looked at me like I had lost my mind and said, "Those are our police escorts, dummy!" I thought, "WOW!

I've never experienced this type of treatment before." We were being treated as if our bus had the President on board. The buses didn't stop for red lights or traffic. The police carved our path through the city while creating a force field of protection around our caravan-like transport. The destination was our home stadium, and the bus driver had total authority to break traffic laws in order to ensure our team would arrive there safely.

In all actuality, it was a short ride from our team hotel to the stadium, but it was executed in such dramatic fashion. The thrill of being glorified by numerous C.U. and Colorado State fans walking to the game and tailgating in various parking lots amplified our collective mood and ego. People were honking at us, waving, yelling, and jumping up and down as the bus rode by. As I looked around at my teammates, it was evident who was getting ready to play in the game, and who was not. There was a silence that divided the freshmen and veterans. The veteran players definitely had a look of determination on their face. I figured, as did most of the freshmen, that I'd better shut up and stay out of everyone's way and just soak everything in.

We entered the locker room and our uniforms were hanging in our lockers, with the game day program that everyone would receive in the stands, along with a stick of gum. Guys were walking around giving high fives, listening to cd players, stretching, and getting taped up. Neuheisel had given our freshman class the option to suit up for the game. Since it was going to be our first experience suiting up, we all decided to do it. As I walked up to my locker I couldn't help but stare at my "#23" game day jersey and visualize everything I was going to someday accomplish in that uniform. And I must admit, I had never looked better in a uniform.

The freshman stood out like sore thumbs, high-fiving, as we strutted around giving dap to one another on how "fly" we looked in our uniforms. The typical rookies!

Over by the locker room door was a game day itinerary on the white board that described the schedule of events right up to kickoff. As the minutes ticked off the clock, bringing kickoff closer to reality, the intensity inside the locker room started to pick up. It was at a supreme level. Our strength and conditioning coach, Doc Kreis, was the most intense as he came around to take one final look in everyone's eyes before we headed out. We gathered in our team room for one final pep talk and prayer, and then IT WAS ON!

Like soldiers marching through the trenches of a combat field, we climbed the stairs out of the athletic facility, and exploded through the doors leading to our game field. We poured out in droves. You could hear thousands of fans cheering and yelling. Excitement overwhelmed each and every one of us as we began screaming and jumping up and down. Doc Kreis managed to bob and weave his way through the line of rowdy players waiting to be unleashed. This was our home turf and we were determined to do everything to defend it. Losing was not an option!

Doc opened the door leading to our team's inflated tunnel. Like wild buffalos, we stampeded our way into this apparatus, and for a moment, we all went deaf from the yelling coming from the crowd, and the noisy motor of the smoke machine pumping vast amounts of smoke into the inflatable tunnel. The smoke was so dense that we were all blinded. We had to feel for the players in front of us. Once our ears adjusted to the noise, Doc yelled out, "Listen for my word!" Like caged animals, we frantically stirred in place, awaiting his declaration. All of a sudden we heard the latch from our mascot's metal cage open, and Doc yelled, GO! Our team emerged through a cloud of thick smoke behind the best mascot in college football, "Ralphie" our team's live buffalo. We converged upon the scene of an Olympic-sized crowd of crazy fans. It felt as if I was hurled back in time, engaging in a battle at the Roman Coliseum. The sensation of it all was more glorious than I had ever imagined. The setting was almost too much to handle. I felt my knees wobble beneath me. I just knew I was going to collapse right then and there. Luckily, my legs did not betray me as I ran down our team's sideline.

We barely won the game that day, but it was a day I will never forget as long as I live. I spent the whole game just soaking in the energy of the atmosphere and of the day's events. From our opponents, to the television cameras, fans, cheerleaders and TV timeouts, it was a spectacle I was privileged to witness. There is nothing like the feeling of having the one thing you desire most within the grasp of your fingertips.

To be able to have it become a reality is a transcending moment of the spirit. I had never felt this "high" in my life! I had never felt more determined and empowered to fulfill my dream. Coming this far was an achievement in and of itself. It is a moment that I hold close to my heart and will never forget. It was truly a surreal day for me, and the rest of my recruiting class. It would be our time to hit the field sooner than we thought. But on that day, the dream of running out during a Big Time College Football game had been fulfilled, whether I was playing or not. This was the day that I realized, DREAMS DO COME TRUE!

CHAPTER 14

Amateurs or Pros?

WHEN WILL EVERYONE stop carrying on the facade that Big Time College Football is still an amateur sport? There is <u>nothing</u> amateur about the six million a year coach Nick Saban brings in coaching the University of Alabama. And there is definitely nothing amateur about the $68 million dollar brand new athletic facility that the University of Oregon just built.

According to Joshua P. Wimmer's article, "Student Athletes or University Slaves," the NCAA Constitution explicitly says "student athletes shall be AMATEURS...and should be protected from exploitation by professional and commercial enterprises." He goes on to say, "The problem with this rule is that it fails to acknowledge that university athletic programs are indeed commercial enterprises!"

The second edition of the *New Riverside Webster's Dictionary* defines a commercial enterprise as "a business organization, relating or engaged in commerce, designed for profit, and supported by advertising." I don't know about you, but that sounds like Big Time College Football to me! Clearly, no one in their right mind can draw parallel lines between Pop Warner, or even high school football, and the definition of commercial enterprise activity. There is clearly no profit or significant advertising taking place at this level of the game. Instead, it's the sport functioning for the development and sake of the children in the community.

But in big business, many find a way to pay bottom dollar for the labor involved in creating the product, and then flip it for a ridiculous price on the consumer end. However, in college football the product is the player, and we can flip the entertainment value associated with that player into a multi-million dollar TV deal.

So where is all of the money going? It seems to me that the reform of football, as an enterprise at the collegiate level, is mandatory. The athletes put on a show and bring in audiences who are willing to spend their money to be entertained. But are the athletes being fairly compensated? It depends on whom you talk to.

There is someone reading this book right now saying, "But the players receive full ride scholarships!" This is true, and a definite blessing in my eyes. But it's still not enough! A full ride scholarship was the same thing they were giving college football players back in the days of Gale Sayers and Jim Brown. But back then, college football was not a multi-billion dollar industry. The media had not had its hands in the game back then like it does now. These days, college players are household names and their jerseys are sold in stores, their likeness shown in video games, and their highlights projected consistently on national television commercials to entice people to watch. Let's face it! College players are commodities. Everyone has received an increased share of the profits as the game has exploded over the years, except the players.

Keep in mind the majority of the college athletes you watch on television are no different than your average college student when it comes down to the money in their pocket. They are broke! There were plenty of nights that my teammates and I did not go out on the town, for the simple fact that we didn't have the money to spend. Even though we had just performed in front of 60,000 people earlier that day, we found ourselves sitting at home all night, playing the college football video game that EA Sports made millions off of, that we just so happen to be in. Ironic huh?

Back in 2006, the recession began to pick up. The NCAA was looking to solve the problem of dwindling funds in the majority of college athletic departments across the country. In many cases, schools were cutting sports programs simply because they could no longer afford to have them. As the NCAA executives looked at various ways to solve this problem, they ended up coming to the conclusion to increase the college football season from eleven to twelve games per year. Hence, as the NCAA got together to brainstorm how to generate more money for college athletic departments across the country, they came up with the brilliant idea to make college football players put in the extra labor, and play another game to increase revenue for struggling athletic departments.

In disagreement with the NCAA's decision, members of the Coalition on Intercollegiate Athletics (a group representing faculty senates at Division 1A Universities) argued, "To ask football players to compete principally in order to generate increased revenues to support sports programs other than football, without identifying substantial added benefits to themselves, would conflict with the principles of amateurism that are the basis of intercollegiate athletics." In laymen terms, the Coalition alleges that the NCAA is exploiting its football players. They are working the football players for profit as if they are professionals, but none of the players are receiving professional checks.

I wish someone could help me understand how it makes sense for football players to produce monies to keep the non-revenue generating sports above water? Adding insult to injury, these football players will continue to receive only the minimum—the same scholarship perks as those athletes who can't hold their own at the ticket booth. In the world of big business, if and when an employee's sales are bolstering the company's profits, as a whole, then she or he will receive compensation in direct proportion to the value they generate for the company. If the employee does not receive compensation for what he or she produces, then the company stands a good chance of not only losing that big-cash-flow employee, but also losing its "ass" in a lawsuit.

A large percentage of college athletic departments would not even exist without their football teams. In a past PBS report, John Wittmore, former President of Texas Tech University, stated that Texas Tech football helps people realize that Texas Tech University even exists. He also went on to say that the football program helps to generate new students and funding for the general school population as well. It's well known that Notre Dame's NBC TV money helps pump millions into general education scholarships for students there.

So a heartfelt salute goes out to all my Division 1A college football players who strap it up every year for a 12-game season, and in some cases, a 13-game season in order to foot the bill for everyone else. Collegiate players are being exploited and there are committee rules and regulations that ensure the profits go to the universities. While these committees argue that the rules are in place to protect the players and to level the playing field for recruiting among competing universities, I challenge that.

If you compare how players are being compensated against the amount of revenue brought in by their performance, you'd call it working for sweatshop wages. We don't have to make these athletes rich, but a little more financial support would go a long way. Even the opportunity for players to be able to go back to the university and get their degree after their career, would be a creative thank you for time served.

So, as we sit back and watch another fabulous college football season, and witness the hoards of fans file into stadiums across the country, remember to ask yourself are these college football players really amateurs, OR ARE THEY PROS?

CHAPTER **15**

Party Animal

EVERY YOUNG MAN faces that point in his life when it's time to grow up! Basically, it's time to sink or swim. For the first time in my life, my parents were not around to help guide my decisions. Independence! Hooray…. It was a prayer answered! Going off to college and being totally on your own with no adult supervision is emancipation at its finest. To go from spending four years in an all-boys Catholic high school, to living in a co-ed, off-campus dorm at 18 was heaven. I was no longer a boy, but a man around young college women, with NO curfew. I looked at college as a whole new world of opportunity.

Once our freshman class got the word that all of us would be redshirting, we became bona fide party animals, and I was at the head of the pack! Coming into the dorm room at 1:30 a.m. was considered an early night for us. Many nights we didn't even come home at all. Since none of us would be scoring touchdowns on the field, the goal was to score *off* the field. It was as if my lifestyle went from zero to sixty, in a matter of days. Things that I never would have imagined doing under my parent's roof were now normal procedure.

I was wild, my freshman class was wild, and the majority of our team was wild. After about the first two months of college, I had totally forgotten that I had a girlfriend back home in the Bay Area. The peer pressure was intense. Try telling your 18-and 19-year-old freshman classmates that you are not going to the party because you want to talk on the phone all night to your high school sweetheart… that doesn't go too far. Needless to say, our relationship didn't last long.

Before I knew it, I was the go-to man for the party scene. Whether it was a football party, sorority party, or fraternity party, I was the one who had the 411 and connections. I could tell you exactly who to call, where to go, and what time you needed to be there. Every single football team— whether it's a college or a professional team—has someone functioning in this coordinator capacity. The interesting thing is that even the coaches know which player is the go to man! It's their job to know so they can funnel all the recruits they really want to that particular player. Remember, the school that can show a recruit the best time is the school that typically gets the recruit to sign on the dotted line. It's definitely not the most ethical practice, but it's the business. The coaches used me like a closer at a car dealership, or like a baseball reliever in the bottom of the ninth inning.

I arrived on campus in Boulder, Colorado with focus on developing a reputation for my play on the football field. Instead, I left Boulder, Colorado with a reputation for my play off the field. I found myself constantly depressed over lack of play on the football field, but the crazy thing is that I didn't even know I was depressed at the time. I had plenty of ways to numb my mental anguish, and sex became my main vice of choice. I had a plethora of women around, and it served me well in keeping my ego inflated.

I thought sleeping with a lot of women was expected of athletes playing football at a very high profile school. It wasn't right, but it was something I got respect for. College is a time of trial and error, and self-discovery for everyone. Looking back on my bedroom exploits, if I would have been as meticulous about covering receivers as I was about covering women, I would have been a first round draft pick.

In retrospect, I see clearly that my potential was *ill-managed* and *ill-applied*. Instead of using my powers for good, I was using my charisma and prowess to captivate women, and cut up off the field. By the time my college career had come to an end, I had slept with well over 100 women. I was unquestionably considered the man on campus. Unfortunately, not so in the game of football!

CHAPTER 16

The Owner/Coach Dilemma

I MUST ADMIT that coaches, schools, and NFL owners have a major dilemma on their hands. My view of the game changed once I was removed from the field. With the eyes of a sideline spectator, it's easy to identify the stumbling blocks for athletes in the business. The recent rash of off-the-field issues that have made media headlines are examples of a business and culture breeding ignorance. Does the talent of a player, and what they can bring to your team on the field, outweigh the potential for harm off the field by players with unaddressed character issues? It's a shame, but this question has never been more relevant than with today's athlete.

It's rare that we find a super-star talent who has not been in some kind of off-the-field trouble. Whatever happened to players like Barry Sanders and Walter Payton? Guys who were considered the game's biggest names at one point in time, but still carried themselves as if they had a mom and dad, and a sense of moral values. We can never discount the fact that many of our country's top young football talent come from major cities like Los Angeles, Houston, and Miami. Areas where many are exposed to the hard-knock-life reality of communities marked by unemployment, street drug sales, poor living conditions, sub-par education, and crime to get from one meal to the next. Not to mention all of the broken parental bonds. How can we expect greatness off the field from our young athletes, when no one is taking the time to heal them from their traumatic upbringings? Education and counseling for the things they have seen and endured, or the false values they have adopted while coming of age, should be mandatory. Especially for athletes! Yet it remains optional. Which has led to many young men slipping through the cracks.

Although just thirty minutes apart, there is a sharp contrast between the lifestyle of a native Compton Californian, and the lifestyle he will enjoy if he chooses to attend UCLA in Westwood. There is definitely a change of attitude that has to come with the change of environment in order to make it a win-win solution, for the athlete and the school.

The players who don't understand the responsibility that comes with "who they've become" eventually make mistakes. There are countless examples of those who fall aimlessly into this category. When a university or an NFL team evaluates a player, they dig deep! They dig deep to see where the player comes from, how he was parented, whom he associated with, and what mistakes he's made thus far. Then they take all that information and weigh it against how great of a player he is on the field. If his on-the-field production outweighs the negatives their research has revealed, he gets the scholarship or the job. But if the negatives outweigh his talent on the field, the decision-makers move on to the next.

Players are constantly being evaluated as players and as people. One night of bad judgment can cost millions from your checking account years later. When you look at what Michael Vick and others like him have lost in contract and endorsement money, it's ridiculous! It could easily be argued that Michael Vick made a $100 million dollar mistake.

Universities and NFL owners are tired of throwing money at damaged goods. Players' off-the-field activities are under a microscope like never before. Even though the NFL is one of the only multi-billion dollar industries that are actually ready and willing to hire *felons*, they don't prefer it. And college institutions are no different.

One coach may believe that a player is just too big of a risk. While another coach may think it's a good risk to take. Regardless, a player's character versus a player's talent is a huge dilemma for many coaches today.

CHAPTER 17

Behind Training Room Doors

INJURIES AND DRUG tests are par for the course when playing high-level football. All football players feel somewhat uneasy around doctors and hospitals. I have never met a football player that made it to a high level of competition and had never been hurt. NEVER! Now, I must say I have been pretty fortunate and blessed during my 19 years on the field. I got out of the game with minor injuries. Outside of a couple of sprained ankles, torn hamstrings, and torn ligaments in both of my thumbs, my body made it out of the game intact. Unfortunately, I can't say the same for many of my counterparts. My roommate, Victor Rogers, had eight surgeries before he even left college and entered the NFL: knee surgery, hand surgery, shoulder surgery, and ankle surgery are just a few of the reconstructions Big Vic has endured. I can vividly remember him in excruciating pain after a long day of getting cut in the hospital. Believe me, it's no joke hearing a grown man yell and cuss in agony! Vic made it very clear to everyone once he was drafted by the Detroit Lions in 2002 it was all about the money, and not his personal well-being anymore.

Drug testing is mandatory at both the university and professional level. At C.U., we were drug tested annually by two different parties: The NCAA would test us for Steroids and other performance-enhancing drugs, while the Big XII would test us for street drugs. It was never really clear what the consequences were for getting caught, because there were different levels of punishment depending on how much of a particular illegal substance was in your urine. And none of the players wanted to ask specific questions about the consequences because inquiring would insinuate drug use.

Whenever the team huddled up at the end of practice, and the trainers started to walk over with their list of wanted players for drug testing, you could almost tell who was guilty by the look on their face. When you are a part of a fraternity as close as a football team, everyone already knows what their teammates are into anyway. You get nervous for your teammate when you know he smokes marijuana or tried steroids, and his name is on the list. I know there were days that my teammates were nervous for me. But guys who may be a little dirty always seem to have ways to wiggle out of trouble. I know I did!

The trainers and doctors for college and professional football teams are equally wrapped up in the culture of the sport and are part of the fraternity culture as the players are. From my experience, it seems as if the players and team trainers form a pretty strong bond, while the coaches and front office tend to cling more to the team doctors. The trainers are the ones on the sidelines at practice every day and the go-to people for daily needs like ice, tape, over-the-counter painkillers, and assistance with rehabbing injuries. So, players and trainers spend a lot of time talking to each other. The trainers are also younger than most of the team doctors, and make it easier for players to confide in trainers about important issues.

At the University of Colorado, as in most Big Time College Programs, the trainers are actually students. So these are people that you see on campus and occasionally party with as well. I've known players who have had relationships with trainers. It is definitely to a player's benefit to get in good with team trainers. I formed great friendships with some of our team trainers and fortunately they had my back in a few different situations that could have hurt my position with the team. Days when I didn't show up for rehab, it was supposed to be reported to the coaching staff but they marked me down as being present. On other occasions, trainers would give me a heads up on a drug test that was approaching so I could take the proper steps to pass the test, or foreworn another player so they could do the same. Many of my teammates and I kept plenty of urine-cleansing products in our lockers just in case our name was indeed picked to pee in cups for all the world to critique! Relationships with the trainers proved priceless.

Once you go pro, you may find yourself in need of a trainer to cover up how serious your injury is during an intense training camp battle. Many guys have lost jobs during a heated position battle because they got injured while the other player was able to stay healthy. Coaches receive injury reports from the team trainers every day after practice. If your name is on that report too often, you might as well start looking for another job. There is a little saying in the industry: "you can't make the club in the tub." This basically means that you may be a fabulous football player, but if you can't stay healthy, no one is going to keep you around long enough to prove it!

Your body is your meal ticket as an athlete. You don't play; you don't EAT! One of my best friends is Donald Strickland; he's Godfather to my second son, and in my opinion, one of the most versatile, yet underrated defensive backs in the NFL from 2003-2011. He never really received his proper recognition in large part due to a stint of injuries dating back to our high school football years together at Riordan High School. Donald was a major part of the Indianapolis Colts AFC Championship run in 2003, playing the safety position. In 2008, he was a valuable part of the San Francisco 49ers secondary as a cornerback, and has also performed well on top-rated defenses with the New York Jets and the San Diego Chargers. There are very few players in the NFL that can switch hit like Donald.

Cornerback requires an immense amount of athletic ability and speed, while safety requires excellent tackling ability and smarts. Donald had both! But just like in Donald's case, injuries in the world of football have always found a way to halt or significantly deter many promising players' careers.

Just ask Bo Jackson, who may have gone down as the greatest running back of all-time, if not for his career ending hip injury. He could have even been the first player in history to be in both the National Football League Hall of Fame and Major League Baseball Hall of Fame. He is still the first player ever to go to the All-Star game in both respective sports. The world will never know how great Bo Jackson was destined to become, but what he did achieve while healthy, is damn incredible.

Many times as a young football player you feel like you are racing against the injury clock. The odds say you will get injured, but everyone wants to reach their goals before the game takes them out!

My sophomore year in college was the year the threat of injury almost put me permanently on the sideline. It was Friday morning and we were set to battle against San Jose State the next day. I was excited to play against San Jose State because I knew many players on their team from back home in the Bay Area. I recall trying to get out of bed that morning and quickly feeling something was drastically wrong. I could not move my left arm at all, and when I tried, the pain was excruciating! How did this sudden paralysis come to be? I yelled for help from my roommate Victor, who was just as baffled as I was at my limp arm. He had to help me put on my shirt and it was clear to the both of us that I needed to be seen by the team trainers immediately. Victor helped to get me up to our team training room to try and find out what the hell was wrong with my arm. I had gone to bed with no discomfort at all, and now was experiencing sharp, shooting pain.

The trainers looked at my arm and were just as puzzled as I had become. They held off on any opinions and quickly called the team doctor, who was in Denver at the time, to schedule time for me to get looked at. The next thing I knew, all the medical people at our team facility were whispering as they whisked me off to the hospital in Denver.

I was a little nervous as I took the ride down to Denver with one of our team trainers. Once we got to the hospital, our team doctor was in the room along with one of the other doctors from the hospital. They advised me to take off my shirt and began to do a bunch of different test on me to check out my range of motion. Once it became obvious to the docs that I didn't have any range of motion, and every time they moved my arm I could barely stand the pain. They called the coaching staff. Now more doctors had entered the room, and began that doctor huddle up in the corner and whisper stuff again.

After the doctors broke their huddle, they approached me with a proposition to take a shot. It would be a cortisone shot, which was explained as a numbing solution to whatever was going on in my arm. The benefits, they explained, would outweigh the limited risks. The biggest benefit I latched onto was the fact that it would allow me to play the next day. Once I heard the shot would help me be able to play against San Jose State, I was all in. The shot was a must! Our head coach, Gary Barnett, had already expressed to me that it was essential I was able to play, due to San Jose States pass happy attack. The docs proceeded to apply some sort of numbing spray on my shoulder, so I wouldn't feel the pain of the biggest needle I had ever seen in my life. Then they injected me with my shot of Cortisone. About one hour later my arm felt as good as new.

Thinking back on the situation, it is interesting to me how they didn't give me a diagnosis of what was wrong with me. Instead, they only discussed how to patch things up. Hmmm! I had no idea what the substance was, or what it could do to me in the long run. I acted naïvely and rash in making my decision. What I didn't know was the fact that cortisone is nothing more than a synthetic steroid that temporarily masks a person's injury. It really does nothing to help heal the injury; it only blocks the mind's ability to decipher it as being in pain. This is very serious. Pain is your body's way of telling you that something is wrong. Although you feel fine, you actually can make the injury worse. Oftentimes with cortisone shots a person will be in worse pain once the shot wears off.

To add insult to injury was the fact that I was only used for nothing more than a few meaningless plays towards the end of our lopsided victory over San Jose State. The next day, the shot wore off and I experienced more pain than I could possibly imagine. I damaged my arm far worse than my original injury by playing in the San Jose State game. I was pissed off and experiencing ridiculous pain in my apartment bedroom. I later learned from my teammate's father, who is a doctor, that most doctors won't administer more than 3 cortisone shots because of the possibility of tendon wear. But I know plenty of guys who sucked it up for the betterment of the team and received 6 to 8 shots in their career just to get through certain games. It may not be the best idea or most ethical way to stay on the field, but it's the reality of what goes on, behind training room doors!

CHAPTER 18

I'm Okay, Coach

ALONG THE JOURNEY to become a professional player, every athlete will quickly realize that it is imperative you learn how to play while hurt, especially in football. Being able to play while hurt is truly the difference in making the team or not making the team, in having a long career, or having a short career. Tim Green, author of *The Dark Side of The Game* wrote, "PAIN AND FOOTBALL ARE INSEPARABLE." And he is absolutely right! After your first contact in a major college or professional training camp, your body will never be at 100% for the rest of the season. I have never heard of a player with a meaningful football career that has never had to fight through pain or injury. It's never a question of whether or not you will get injured. The real question is when, and how bad?

The one phrase that has been deeply ingrained into every Big Time Football player's mindset is the phrase, "I'm okay, coach!" I have heard myself saying it on many occasions, even when it was completely the opposite case. Through torn hamstrings, dislocated fingers and torn ligaments in both of my thumbs, I have recited this mantra. The *fear* of losing your job is not just an emotion, it's a reality. Whether you are a college senior, trying to keep some hot shot freshman or sophomore from taking your position, or you are an NFL veteran whose team just drafted a first round draft pick at your position, losing your job is always one play away!

You find that your tolerance for pain increases under certain circumstances, such as self-preservation and taking care of your family. Just ask

Drew Bledsoe, the former NFL quarterback who retired in 2007, after having three young, up-and-coming quarterbacks on three different teams take his job throughout his career. We would have never heard of a future NFL Hall of Famer by the name of Tom Brady if it wasn't for the violent hit Drew Bledsoe took against the Jets in 2001, which caused internal bleeding. Legends have been made off of other player's injuries.

The second reason many football players hug close to the phrase "I'm okay, coach" is for the respect of their fellow teammates. Being hurt and fighting through the pain to help your team win a game are the things legends do. It holds the kind of weight in the locker room that an old war veteran story does. Where the solider has been shot three times and still finds a way to go back into the line of fire and save his comrades. Everybody has heard the football stories where the star player gets injured early in the playoff game or the Super Bowl and has to leave the game. Then, in a miraculous turn of events, the star is able to return when the game is all but lost and lead his team to victory and infamy. The fear of losing personal respect from one's teammates always has and always will make a football player put fighting through pain and injury before his own personal safety!

Many guys don't find out how injured they really are until the end of the season. And by then there has already been extensive damage done to their body. An athlete will quickly realize that time is very precious, especially at the professional level. One thing coaches and owners do not have is the virtue of patience. There is no such phrase in Big Time Football that says, "let's win later!" Everything is built around NOW! That includes your contract or scholarship. So what does that mean for athletes? It means if you want to keep your job, you stay on the field by any means necessary! The sport is too competitive to sit out for a long period of time. You must, and will, be replaced if you are not able to play.

When once asked, "What is his motivation behind such a tremendous off-season workout program?" Jerry Rice, the best receiver to ever catch a football answered, "I always felt as though someone was trying to take my job." And he was right! To his credit, he held off many failed attempts. Until finally, age, and the destiny of a man named Terrell Owens, sent the best receiver of all-time packing his bags for the Oakland Raiders. But hey! That's the nature of the game.

You fight to take another's job, until eventually someone takes yours! If you are injured all the time you will just speed up the inevitable. A kid at a Big Time Football school (like Ohio State or USC) may never get the chance to see the dream of playing professional football come true if he experiences too many injury issues in college. Many professional players play through injuries just to avoid the, "he's always hurt" label. That label has cost numerous players money and opportunities for jobs. Trust me. Most football players don't love cortisone shots, painkillers, alcohol, and street drugs. It becomes an acquired love that takes away the pain and stress of the game they play.

Let's put you in the driver's seat for a minute. Let's say you were able to provide a beautiful home for your wife, great schools for your kids, and retirement for your parents through your fortune acquired by playing ball. But, all of those things are now in jeopardy because you are not able to perform through the pain. Would receiving a shot of cortisone, or popping a few Vicodin pills before a game, be a hard decision for you? That's the question these guys are faced with on a daily basis in the world of Big Time Football.

It's the lifestyle we have chosen. The pain is just the consequence we deal with. Anything worth having always comes with a price. Especially when it's your dream!

CHAPTER 19

Recruiting From the Inside Out

ASK ANY COMPETITIVE athlete playing in a team sport what their main priority is and I guarantee you the response will be to <u>win</u>. A student athlete's job is not over once he signs a letter of intent. It is made clear to all scholarship athletes that they will also be called upon to assist the coaching staff in attracting the nation's top talent to their school. This is what I like to call, "recruiting from the inside out." This was also my first introduction into sales. All the players were taught to sell both the University of Colorado and our football program to the best of our abilities. Boundaries were never discussed and limits were never set. And what our school wasn't willing to do, believe me the next school would. So you do whatever it takes to close the deal! Did we have private parties? Yes. Did we have recruits around strippers and strip clubs? Yes. But once again, this is the culture of the sport. This is not something unique to C.U., this is a practice employed at universities across the United States.

I guess you could say that Big Time College Football is fraternity life on steroids! College coaches are great at pairing up the right recruits with the right players who can close the deal. Many times a recruit can figure out how he is perceived by the school recruiting him, by who they have host him on his recruiting trip. Let's say you are a highly rated high school receiver and you take a trip to the University of Texas A&M. If the Texas A&M coaching staff has Johnny Manziel—their Heisman Trophy-winning quarterback, host you on your trip, that is definitely going to leave a lasting impression on you. On the contrary, if your host is a red-shirt freshman with no clout, then the trip is less likely to leave the recruit eager to return. Even though my name didn't hold as much weight as Johnny Manziel, I did pride myself on doing a pretty good job of recruiting for our program. The majority of recruits under my watch at C.U. actually did end up committing to our school.

In fact, out of my five-year service of selling our program, only three players that I hosted didn't sign with our school. The first two, Andrae Thurman and Bobby Wade were two receivers out of Arizona who visited the University of Colorado back in 1998 after our Hula Bowl victory over Oregon. Both players were very talented and had a fabulous time during their C.U. recruit weekend. I believe both of them actually committed at first to C.U., but we had some coaching changes after their recruiting trip and ultimately, both players decided to go to the University of Arizona instead. Cleary, this was a big loss for our program given that both Andrae and Bobby ended up going to the NFL. Andrae as a free agent to the N.Y. Giants and Bobby Wade, a fifth round pick of the Bears, had a seven-year NFL career. Bobby actually finished his college career as the University of Arizona's all-time leading receiver.

But the third recruit I lost happened to be a "big fish"! The *One* who could have changed the course of our football program for a couple of years. I don't care to mention this player's name because we actually lost out to the school he chose because of some illegal activity. Our team was in need of a big time tailback at the time, so when this player came up for his recruiting trip, the coaches made it well known that he was definitely a player they wanted. So of course, they chose me to host him.

I was the player who could show anyone a good time if they wanted to get a feel for the social life at the University of Colorado. Once I got a hold of this player, we hit it off right from the beginning. He actually had such a great time on his recruiting trip that he did, in fact, commit to C.U., and everybody was happy. About two weeks later, our coaching staff got word that this tailback decided to change his commitment to a school in the S.E.C. Our coaching staff promptly asked me to get in contact with this particular player to find out why he had a change of heart. During our phone conversation, I became intrigued by a string of events that led him to change his decision. After affirming that he was sold on the University of Colorado, and truly believed that he was going to become a Buffalo, he revealed information that made my jaw hit the floor. A school in the S.E.C. made him a proposition that he, nor his family, could refuse. Thirty grand later, this big fish swam into another sea. By the way, this is a school that has recently been accused of giving a big name NFL quarterback money while he attended their school, as well.

But, when you come from a family with very little or modest financial income, the decision is clear cut which way to go. Ultimately, the school in the S.E.C. that "won" the running back's services, made a wonderful financial investment. They went to a B.C.S. Bowl game, and the tailback enjoyed a very successful NFL career. Although the recruitment was illegal and morally questionable, to some degree, it ironically resulted in being a win-win for the player and the school involved.

After my conversation with this player, I told him I couldn't blame him for his decision. I wished him the best of luck and told him that if he changed his mind, the University of Colorado would still love to have him. Then, I went back into our team's headquarters and told our coaching staff that I couldn't get in contact with him!

CHAPTER 20

The Recruitment of Donald Strickland

THE RECRUITMENT OF Donald Strickland, my best friend, was by far the most interesting experience of my "recruiting from the inside out" experience. Donald Strickland was one of my former teammates at Riordan High School in San Francisco. He was one hell of a safety and running back in high school, but lacked the prototypical size to stay at those positions in college. Coach Neuheisel and the Colorado coaching staff thought Donald would make an excellent cornerback. Donald was one year behind me at Riordan. So I was a freshman at C.U. when he was a senior at Riordan. Considering the fact that I played quarterback at Riordan and received a Division 1A football scholarship, I was definitely someone that Donald looked up to as a player and someone he could get advice from during his recruiting process.

In addition, we were already good friends in high school, but our relationship really began to blossom through our phone contact my freshman year in college. Donald is a very smart guy, and as I stated before, if you want to get somewhere in life you have to link up with someone who has already been there. During my freshman year at Colorado, Donald and I would talk on a weekly basis. I could tell he was on a mission to play at a major college level by the questions he would ask and the enthusiasm in his voice.

Soon the word started getting back to our coaching staff at Colorado about the big games Donald was having back at Riordan. About mid way through my freshman year, our coaching staff wanted to indeed offer Donald a scholarship. Words can't express the level of excitement I felt thinking about the possibility of playing once again with my close friend and high school teammate. UCLA and Cal were two other schools that were in hot pursuit of Donald's talents as well. But the University of Colorado felt pretty strong about our chances to land Donald because they could use me as the "X-Factor". After Donald's last high school game was over, he scheduled his recruiting trip to Colorado to come spend some time with his boy and visit the campus. Obviously, considering our background, I was the logical choice to be Donald's player host on his recruiting trip. My only job was to show Donald a good enough time to make him commit to becoming a Buffalo. But sometimes things are not always as easy as you would think they should be.

Big Vic and I had a great weekend planned for Donald's trip. As Mother Nature would have it, it began snowing the day Donald came out to Boulder, Colorado. This was no deterrent for Vic and me because we lived by the credo, "as long as there's alcohol and college women around, you can always manage to stay warm!"

Since Donald was only going to be in town for a couple of days we didn't have any time to waste. Yeah, having his friend at the school he was considering was a plus for Donald, but that wasn't going to be enough. Victor and I still needed to sell Donald on "why" he should go to the University of Colorado. For this occasion, I had to reach deep into my little black phone book to pick the right woman for the occasion. Only in college do you hear certain things come out of a girl's mouth that will stick in your mind, like the first time you heard your parents say a curse word. I would always make a mental note of what certain women had said to me in the past. And one woman's name in particular kept jumping to the foreground of my mind when preparing for Donald's trip. Her name was Tiffany (name has been changed to protect privacy).

We met a few months prior to Donald's recruiting trip, at a Halloween party. She looked amazing that night. I never really did know her official ethnicity, but picture a Pacific Islander girl with curves in all the right places, wearing a sexy black cat suit, that perfectly hugged every inch of her body. She epitomized Hale Berry in body and face, but with a Polynesian twist. Think of the movie, *Cat Woman,* starring Ms. Berry, and you've got exactly the image you need.

As I got to know Tiffany in the months leading up to Donald's trip, it became very clear that this girl was not shy at all when it came to talking about sex. It actually seemed as if it was her favorite subject.

There was no one more befitting to get the job done. Tiffany would be the enchantress ordained to mystify and spellbind Donald into Colorado's football program.

It was extremely cold that night and the roads were too slick to drive to our favorite downtown party destinations. Instead, we found ourselves drinking, and playing John Madden Football all night until Tiffany came over. With a quick and informal introduction, Tiffany entered and took a seat on my bed as we continued to play the game. Donald really didn't think too much of it, but my roommate Vic and I knew what was about to go down. We needed Donald to commit, and Tiffany was the ace up our sleeve. Due to the nature of what happened next, and the audience this book is intended for, I'm going to refrain from talking about what happened next, but I will say everyone in attendance had a memorable night working for the program.

Even as tantalizing as Tiffany was, she was not the deciding factor in Donald's decision to come to C.U. There was pressure from all sides for Donald to attend UCLA and play ball there. He shared with me that he had an equally good recruiting trip with all the bells and whistles that C.U. had displayed. And who can argue with going to school in Westwood? More importantly, he had an uncle who played ball at UCLA and was pushing him to carry on the family tradition. Donald was teetering back and forth, when it started to become clear to me that he was headed for the Bruin's lair. This was the point at which it seemed like all bets were off.

I was not particularly fond of losing talent to other schools, and I sure wasn't about to let my boy get away. I knew to get the truth about which school he was leaning towards, I would have to talk to Donald's mother, Gwen. One night, she and I were on the phone and she said, "you know, Terry (the name everyone back home used for me), the real reason Donald is not sure about Colorado is because Donald is not sure he wants to compete with YOU!"

I remember things getting silent for a moment on the phone. The thought of having to compete with my good friend had never crossed my mind. I suddenly threw that scenario out of my head and then went back into sales mode. I told Donald's mother that there are two cornerbacks on the field at one time. I began to sell her and Donald on the idea that we would never have to compete for the same position, given the fact that we would play on opposite sides of the field. At least that's what was told to me!

Naïve, just a freshman, and new to the culture of Big Time College Football, it was unfathomable to me that the coaching staff would actually pit two friends (who were like brothers) against each other. I reasoned with myself that there might be more than one cornerback on the field 99% of the time during a football game. Yet, I forgot to note that there is only room for one number "#1" cornerback on a team. In the game of *Football* you are always in competition and never forget that! Nonetheless, we ended up getting Donald to sign on the dotted line with the University of Colorado. It was official. And after that day things would never be the same. But there is never growth without change. And only time would tell if the love between best friends would be stronger than our love for the game!

CHAPTER 21

Scholarship Donors

THERE ARE ALWAYS plenty of people behind the scenes that help make the show go on in entertainment. These invisible people in the world of college football are known as a collective group called, scholarship donors. Scholarship Donors do exactly what the name implies. University alumni and friends of the program actually foot the bill for the football players' scholarships. I had always assumed that if the University was offering me my scholarship, then it would be paying for it too. Boy, was I far off the mark in my assumption. It is in fact the scholarship donors who cut the big checks to make sure that your books, and dorm-room are taken care of. These scholarship donors are mostly people who just want to be involved with the football program and the athletic department. They want the opportunity to be affiliated with something. There's no better way to become a part of something than to invest in it.

If athletic departments want to raise money, the scholarship donors are the first to receive sales calls. The official name of the University of Florida Football field is not the "swamp." It's the "Ben Hill Griffin Stadium at Florida Field". "The Griffins" are very well known for making their fortune in the citrus and cattle industries. CNNMoney.com reported that the Griffins have donated well over $20 million to the University of Florida athletic department since the 1980's. The same CNNMoney. com article also reported that the University of Florida soccer stadium, baseball complex and aquatic center were all bankrolled by some of the University's most distinguished donors.

During the 2006-2007 athletic seasons, the University of Florida became the first school in NCAA history to have its football team and basketball team both win the National Championships at the Division 1A level.

The University of Oregon cashes in on the checks of probably the most well known donor in college sports: Phillip H. Knight, co-founder and chairman of Nike. Mr. Knight is a large contributor to the University of Oregon's football prominence. Mr. Knight and his wife Penny, donated $100 million in August 2007 to the University of Oregon football program, which paid its dividends in 2011 when the team played in it's very first National Championship game. Donations like that will automatically ensure that Oregon football will stay competitive for years to come.

The recent $68 million football facility built in 2013, is also funded by Knight, and is regarded by most to be the best athletic facility in the college and pro ranks. It's no different than the old adage, "if you build it they will come." The top high school talent will always follow magnificent facilities. If 80% of your time in college is going to be spent training, wouldn't you want to be in a top-flight training facility?

Players have been the beneficiaries of donor compensation, both on and off the record, for years. Whether it was the players who got busted back in the "Oklahoma Sooner" hey days, or the recruit I hosted who got paid to play in the S.E.C., money-changing hands in football usually makes big things happen on the field.

It has been said that donor's money is the best money because it's usually the hardest to trace. I know players who have had cash deposited anonymously into their checking accounts, as well as players who have had their wives receive thousands of dollars for delivering babies during player's college years. Scholarship donors are also notorious for providing well-paid summer jobs for some athletes. In the NCAA's eyes, it's all wrong! But personally, knowing the financial situations of those players at that time, I can say that the money they received was definitely needed, and right on time. Especially when you consider the fact that many of these players brought in millions to the University's football program.

A scholarship donor might just be the person to invite you into his home to provide you with a nice home-cooked meal, or graciously swing by your dorm room with a nice comforter and sheets, so you don't have to spend your last $60 dollars left in your little college checking account.

Technically, it's illegal to the NCAA, but it seems morally correct to me considering the work these athletes do on the field. At some point, they deserve a piece of this multi-million dollar pie given they bring the show to life. In some cases, the power of the mighty donor extends into influencing staff members as well. They have the loudest voices in coaching decisions for certain programs. Why do you think coaches make sure they are in attendance at all of their alumni and fundraising events? The more money a donor is willing to donate, the more their opinions are valued. Believe me, no coach or athletic department wants to burn bridges with prestigious scholarship donors and alums. It would literally cost too much!

CHAPTER 22

Where is the loyalty?

FAST FORWARD TO 1998. Our team had just beaten the University of Oregon in the 1998 Hula Bowl. Oregon had the future number three overall pick in the upcoming NFL Draft, Akili Smith. We all proudly converged into the locker room feeling as though we had set the tone for our next season. Our ear-to-ear smiles and excitement were by no means inspired by the great Bowl victory we had just completed. The excitement was cultivated by the thought of how great the future of the Colorado Buffalo football team looked. There was a prophetic feeling of colossal opportunity heading in our team's direction. Our team was so young and so talented, that the sky was the limit. We all walked around that post-game locker room feeling that the 1999 season had the potential to be a season none of us would ever forget.

Coach Neuheisel added fuel to the fire when, during his postgame speech, he urged us to go home and enjoy our New Year's holiday, but come back to school ready to work, because in 1999, the Colorado Buffaloes should not expect anything less than a NATIONAL CHAMPIONSHIP! The locker room erupted with excitement. Not only did a National Championship sound good, our team truly believed we could pull it off! Unfortunately what our team didn't know at the time was that it would be the last time Rick Neuheisel would ever address our team as our head coach. Less than two weeks later, Neuheisel had abandoned our team to become the head coach for the University of Washington Huskies.

I got back on the plane to head home feeling good about the team I was a part of. Since the game was played on Christmas day, we actually had a good two weeks at home with our families until we were due back in Colorado for the second semester of school, and winter conditioning. I headed home as a 19-year-old local celebrity. These two weeks would be a perfect time to catch up with family and friends, and to party.

One night I walked into my parents' home at about 10:30 p.m. after spending some time with some high school friends, and received the biggest shock of my young football career. My dad was up in his room watching television in bed as usual, when I went in his room to let him know I was home. At that time my father came right out and told me, "your coach just left Colorado!" This sort of comment wasn't something my dad was above joking about, so I brushed it off initially, and told him to stop playing. But the look on his face was not what usually followed after one of his typical pranks. He instructed me to watch the 11:00 p.m. edition of Sports Center on ESPN. That's when our home phone started to ring, one call after the other.

The word had gotten out, so family and friends were beginning to call to see if we had heard of my coach's departure. In my room, I turned on the TV and prayed for this all to be a bad dream... Nightmare confirmed! Headlines stated that head coach, Rick Neuheisel, had indeed jumped ship for the University of Washington. Grief overcame me, and then anger took the helm. I was pissed off!

It felt like being cheated on by a lying spouse. A spouse that says all the right things, makes you feel like you are the only one, but is so calculated with their affairs, that when the facts are placed in front of you about their deception, you literally get sick to your stomach.

To make matters worse, he didn't even have the decency to tell us in person—we had to find it out through the media circus. Every news and sports channel had a segment on Rick Neuheisel's departure. I felt so low. Rick himself had romanced me and all the other guys on the team, so to speak: extravagant dinners, parties, promises of greatness, and victory together. And just like that, he and our collective athletic dreams had disappeared. In the heat of the moment of betrayal, how do you rationalize something like this? I couldn't! There would be lessons learned later on, but for now, it was betrayal in the first-degree and what did this mean for my future?

But it wasn't all bad, however. This taught me a very valuable lesson about making life decisions. This was a lesson that will help aspiring athletes at all levels of the game ask themselves the "why," before signing with one school or professional team versus another.

First, and foremost, a coach should *never* be the sole purpose in your signing decision! A coach's contract is *no* stronger than the paper that it is written on. I was so excited about performing for, and learning under coach Neuheisel, that I let his charm whisk me away into a fantasy without giving any weight to the possibility of his early-rumored departure.

The University of Colorado Buffaloes was about to venture into unchartered waters. We didn't have a head coach, which meant there was definitely going to be change. Unexpected change can always be a source of stress and discouragement, and the future of our team and my career were up in the air. I was only a red-shirt freshman at the time, which meant unless the "big heads" who were in control of hiring our next head coach hired someone already on our coaching staff; I would be playing the next 75% of my college career under a person I have never even met before. Not to mention, I had coaxed my best friend, Donald Strickland, to come along for the journey. He was a true freshman, so he had not even hit the field yet! Which meant 100% of his career was up for grabs.

So excuse my French, but at the time, I was thinking we were definitely "screwed!" Coach Neuheisel had made a personal business decision that would affect all of us, and possibly our personal dreams, plus the team's dreams as well.

The true intensity of this betrayal hit when we realized that Neuheisel's entire career moves took place behind the scenes, right under our noses while we were in Hawaii for the Hula Bowl. During the 1998 Bowl season, our team had accepted a bid to play against the Oregon Ducks, but this particular year, the representatives for the game thought it would be a great idea to have the first ever, Bowl double-header! I'm sure the Hula Bowl committee didn't think at the time that adding another game might eventually change the landscape of college football and the futures of so many individual players, but it did!

Usually teams spend a week at the Bowl site before the game to get used to the venue, the city, get extra practice, and get involved with pre-Bowl festivities. All of this is in the name of publicity. It helps to attract local and national attention to the game. Since the Hula Bowl was hosting the first ever double-header Bowl game in college football history, all of our pre Bowl game events included four teams instead of the usual two.

Barbara Hedges, the athletic director for the University of Washington at the time, was in attendance in Hawaii to support her Huskies, scheduled to play the Air Force Academy that year. This Hawaii trip also afforded Ms. Hedges the opportunity to take a good look at a prospective new head coach for her Huskies. So we can assume that the whole week our team was in Hawaii, Barbara Hedges and Rick Neuheisel were plotting what would be the biggest coaching change in college football for the upcoming season. I guess we will never really know if coach Neuheisel's post-game locker room vision—of pursuing a conference and National Championship—was sincere or not. Or if he already knew that this vision was not going to include him?

CHAPTER 23

Team Confusion and Tough Decisions

MY RETURN TO what had once been a dream come true was now lack-luster and depressing. The Buffaloes, once powerful and conquering, had been essentially slaughtered and left for roadside vulture meat. Everyone from our athletic director to the custodians was in shock and dismay. The players were all walking around as if they were toddlers in a department store who had just lost mommy. And the rumors were rampant. It just seemed like no one had any sense of direction. Everything got put on the back burner. Our program was severely interrupted. Our winter conditioning was delayed; our recruitment of prospects was lazily executed. It was a nightmare! Doc Kries, our strength and conditioning coach, became the glue that held our team together. Doc leaned heavily on some of the upper classmen to keep control of things behind the locker room doors. It crossed my mind to explore my options of transferring to another school, and many of my teammates pondered that possibility as well. If it weren't for the leadership of the veterans on our team, we would have disbanded and left the program without hope at all. Instead, we stuck together in our time of crisis. As a result, our adversity made us stronger as individuals and as a team.

Rick Neuheisel recruited all my roommates, Victor Rogers, Jashon Sykes, and Donald Strickland. Victor and I were red-shirt freshman, while Jashon and Donald were true freshman. One night, to our surprise, we got a call from none other than Mr. Neuheisel himself. He wanted to explain his decision to all of us and wish us the best of luck. It was later revealed to us by the NCAA that the phone conversation we had with Neuheisel was considered a violation.

The NCAA believed that Neuheisel might have been trying to coerce some of us to switch over to the University of Washington. They found it suspicious that he contacted a group of his hand-picked freshman recruits that had plenty of college eligibility left to spare. But the truth of the matter was that there was no foul play involved. Despite what many think, Neuheisel actually had a HEART! But the NCAA quickly reacted, banning transfer of any Colorado players to the University of Washington. This ban was not completely successful however.

Taylor Barton, a true-freshman quarterback on our team, transferred to the UW after a brief junior college pit stop, to disenfranchise himself from the University of Colorado. Weeks had passed since Neuheisel's decision was made public. "Coach Neu" even paid us a visit to address our team one last time. This took some serious balls, on his part. I kept thinking just how much courage he had stored up to dare show his face back in Dal Ward. Our entire team had gathered in our large meeting room. As I looked around the room, looks of disgust filled everyone's face. Boy, if looks could kill, Neuheisel would have exhausted all nine lives just like a cat, that day. At the age of 19, I can't say I had ever been in a room filled with as much tension and frustration as this! If I were Neuheisel I would have had a damn security guard right alongside me. But he didn't. Neuheisel addressed the team in his usual calm and collected fashion and kept it short and sweet. Very humbly, he spoke of how tough his decision was and how he loved us, and wished us the best of luck.

Before he could exit, Neuheisel asked if anyone wanted to say something. Everyone was silent. You could have heard a pin drop! Then Tyler Gregorak, one of my fellow teammates, said, "see you September 25th!" Neuheisel knew exactly what he meant, and nodded his head in agreement, and then walked out.

Everyone knows that college football schedules are planned years in advance. No one could imagine our coach would leave, and in doing so would create one of the largest rivalries in college football for the next two years. As luck would have it, we had a home and away series with the Huskies from Washington starting that upcoming year, and September 25th was CIRCLED, UNDERLINED, and WRITTEN IN RED on our team's master game schedule in our meeting room. Whether guys admitted it or not, we all marked off days on our calendars leading up to the game. September 25th would be the day the Buffaloes sought revenge. But before our team could capture sweet revenge we still needed to find Rick Neuheisel's replacement.

CHAPTER 24

Introducing Gary Barnett

OUR TEAM STARTED winter conditioning for the 1999 season with no head coach. Our strength and conditioning coach, Doc Kries, was in control of the football team. It's amazing how he was able to focus on our team, without fully knowing if his own job was secure with our football program. When a brand new head coach is hired, everyone is on pins and needles to see how their own personal situation will be affected, coaches and players alike. There were so many rumors being spread around our athletic department about the university's head coaching search. Most don't know that the university's first pick for the job was Gary Kubiak, the former head coach of the Houston Texans. Our team was overwhelmed with excitement about the possibility of being led by coach Kubiak. At the time of our coaching dilemma, coach Kubiak was the offensive coordinator for the Denver Broncos, under Mike Shanahan. His NFL track record and successes were public record and noteworthy. The promise of Gary Kubiak as head coach brought direct NFL connections to Boulder's hopeful and aspiring professional ball players. Every college player's dream is to play for a coach with big-time NFL connections.

However, our vision of Gary Kubiak as the replacement for Neuheisel was crushed when he decided to pull his name out of the running at the last minute. The Denver Broncos had made it to the Super Bowl that year and coach Kubiak felt inclined to stay with his team.

It was late January and our program was losing ground fast with all of the potential high school and junior college recruits across the country. They'd begin signing with various colleges and universities during the first week in February, so time was of the essence. No prospect would sign with a coach-less football program. At least no top prospect would. Neuheisel had left us behind in the fourth quarter, and we needed someone who was ready to throw a "HAIL MARY." That person ended up being none other than Northwestern University's head coach, Gary Barnett.

Our team was somewhat familiar with his name but he wasn't the popular choice in comparison to Gary Kubiak. Nevertheless, Barnett was no newcomer to C.U. During the Coach McCartney era, Barnett was an assistant on the team that helped Colorado win its first and only National Championship in 1990.

"Praise the Lord," we thought. "We finally have a head coach!" Relief quickly turned to stress once Barnett took the wheel. What we quickly came to realize is that the ghost of Neuheisel would come to haunt us. To understand just how difficult our team's transition was, it is essential to comprehend the history between Rick Neuheisel and Gary Barnett. And oh yes, they definitely had history!

It was pretty well documented that coach Barnett was not fond of coach Neuheisel. After helping to bring home the National Championship for CU, Barnett was overlooked as the successor to McCartney who retired in 1995. Neuheisel was awarded with the position instead. According to popular script, Barnett was sorely disappointed losing out to a young hot-shot with only one year of service at C.U. Barnett felt he deserved this coveted position after putting in eight hard years of service under McCartney. The "big wig" alumni and athletic director decided to go with the young, innovative Rick Neuheisel for the position. Needless to say, coach Barnett felt disrespected by the entire situation.

By 1999, He was already the head coach at Northwestern University, but as I said before, football coaches are very ambitious. Once coach Barnett inherited the reigns to his dream job back at C.U., there was an overwhelming belief around our locker room that Barnett wanted to make sure that none of Rick Neuheisel's fingerprints were left on the program.

From the perspective of a player, a coaching change is like gaining a stepfather after you've become old enough to develop a strong sense of self and family. The disruption is further disquieting when you realize that this stepfather is the polar opposite of your biological father.

Rick Neuheisel was young, creative, and believed in having fun in college, and performing as a football player was icing on the cake! In stark contrast, Gary Barnett was deliberate, by the book, and took more of a "my way or the highway" approach to our team and the people around him. With Neuheisel, we could go skiing, with Barnett we couldn't. With Neuheisel our team emerged from a tunnel filled with smoke before every home game. This ritual disappeared with Barnett. With Neuheisel we were surprised with ice cream on the field after practice. Barnett abandoned this custom as well. Everything our team knew from the previous three years of Rick Neuheisel's tenure gradually became history, and none of us were thrilled about the change.

High Hopes is an autobiographical account written by Gary Barnett that chronicles his time coaching at Northwestern University. Barnett shares his experience at Northwestern and the difficulties he faced with many of the players already recruited by the previous coaching staff. In his book, Barnett asserts that his success at Northwestern would not happen until his own recruits became starting players and shareholders in his improbable vision of excellence.

This was the same philosophy Barnett applied to our Colorado program. He made it clear that the players that accepted his philosophies would be the players who stuck around. Coach Barnett would constantly chime, "I'm going to be here for the next 18 years so you'd better get used to doing things my way!" So I learned that I was going to have to fight for every little bit of playing time I would receive for the rest of my college career.

Loyalty between coaches and players is out the door during a coaching change. If a coach didn't personally recruit you or draft you to his team, he could really care less whether you conform to his views or not. YOU CAN EASILY BE REPLACED by someone he has invested time and research in selecting!

The 1999 season was one of the biggest team disappointments that I have ever endured in my football career. Coach Neuheisel was not off-base in believing that our team should prepare for a National Championship in 1999. Barnett was definitely not inheriting a "work in progress". The shelves were fully stocked by Rick Neuheisel with some of the top recruits from around the country, and handfuls of future NFL draft picks. From day one, there was major division between our team and coach Barnett. There was no way to be successful if minds were not in accord with each other.

You expect growing pains when there are new rules and philosophies being put into place. Unfortunately, our team never came together during Barnett's first year. Our season opener in 1999, against Colorado State, at Mile High Stadium in Denver, Colorado, proved this. The scene was one of mayhem as sideline arguments between players and coaches ensued. Our loyal fans were disgusted with our on-field performance and sideline antics. It was an absolute disaster. The end result being a flat out embarrassment, with a loss of 41-14 by a less talented opponent! It was apparent our team had some things to figure out. But with our "revenge game" against our former coach quickly approaching, we knew we had to figure things out fast!

CHAPTER **25**

Colorado vs. Neuheisel

BY FAR THE biggest game of our 1999 season was our matchup against our former head coach, Rick Neuheisel, and the University of Washington Huskies. Our promise of greatness had been derailed, and here they were rubbing it in, almost flaunting coach Neuheisel in our faces. REVENGE was ours!

The media added fuel to our already blazing fire. The game between Colorado and Washington was publicized the entire off-season, and tabbed in the pre-season as must-see TV in college football. Every time our team picked up a magazine or watched a college football show, we had to see our former coach wearing the purple and gold of the Washington Huskies.

ABC sent Dan Fouts and the legendary Keith Jackson, to commentate the game against Washington that year. They were the "A-Team" of commentators for ABC. Every college football player in the country wakes up on Saturday game days and turns on ESPN to watch "college game day." The University of Colorado holds a special place in its heart for the college game day crew, considering Chris Fowler, one of the show's co-hosts, was an alumni of the University of Colorado. But that day there were about four different channels previewing our game as the headlining event.

During the pre-game press conference, Neuheisel recalled being in all of the Buffalo players' homes to recruit them, as he watched coach's film to prepare for our game. He knew each of our strengths and weaknesses on an individual basis. Indeed, this was a rare advantage for any coaching staff to have, going into battle.

On paper we were easily the more talented and dominant team. Neuheisel knew our team was fast because he built our team that way. But he also knew we were undersized in many positions, especially on the defensive side of the ball. He figured the only chance that Washington would have to win the game would be to get physical with us.

While our talent appeared grand, in reality there was much for us to be fearful about. This was only the fourth game of the season, and the new order of Gary Barnett was still a work in progress as proven by our sub-par performances up to this point. Washington also had the home field advantage for our first meeting with our old coach. Not to mention, Husky Stadium is well known for being one of the loudest stadiums in college football, the 75,000-seat venue was built with the intention to keep sound locked inside.

All week in practice our coaches blasted fake crowd noise through huge stereo speakers and made us practice with hand signals in anticipation that we would not be able to communicate on the field once the game started. We had a large alumni and fan following heading out to the game that year and many well wishers from the school. Even though many of the regular students and fans had never met Neuheisel a day in their life, their resentment towards him was inherent. The single overwhelming motivation felt by our team was to prove to Neuheisel that he had made the WRONG decision to leave us!

As we approached the stadium in our chartered buses, you could see thousands of fans decked out in purple and gold, migrating towards the stadium to get ready for the showdown. One of the unique things about Husky Stadium is that it is very close to Union Bay, on Lake Washington. Some of the more affluent fans and alumni arrive at the stadium in boats and yachts. This is really one of the great scenes of college football.

During pre-game warm-ups, we were greeted by heckling Husky fans making jokes about our former coach leaving our school. My roommate, Big Vic, was one of the most famous recruits ever to come out of the state of Washington. In many fans' eyes he was looked upon as a traitor! This really brought out the ugly in the Husky crowd. He had to endure some of the nastiest taunts for the duration of warm ups. It was hard to stay focused during our position drills; the pre-game time seemed to disappear quickly.

Then it was time to get it on! There was plenty of hard hitting and trash talking throughout the entire game. I can recall one special teams play spilling over into the Washington sidelines where we shamelessly admonished our former coaching staff for abandoning us. I personally cut Neuheisel down to size with my truant stare when we made eye contact during the game. If I were close enough, harsh words would have followed my lack of physical courtesy and respect. However, there was a game in full throttle and there was no time for drama.

There was never a moment of domination for either team. It was any-one's game. The back and forth battle finally came to a close with an un-expected outcome for Colorado. Having a chance to tie the game late in the 4th quarter, our offense was unable to convert on a big 4th-down play. We ended up losing to the University of Washington that day, 24-31. In the end, Neuheisel had won. As we watched the Washington Huskies run onto the field after the game, our team couldn't help but feel our hearts sink.

Feelings that Neuheisel got over on us again became increasingly dif-ficult to get out of my mind. Defeat caused us all to man up as Neuheisel approached the middle of the field to shake hands. That's when the unex-pected happened for me. Finally face to face with my old coach, I wanted to let him have it. Instead, he said something that would change the focus of my energy from anger to forgiveness.

His words and demeanor were sincere as he said, "You have always been one of my favorite players… keep fighting." I got the feeling that he was both happy and sad to beat us. I said goodbye yet again to the coach who convinced me to sign on the dotted line for CU. Feeling conflicted by the emotional and physical battle that was fueled by my anger, I realized that my anger was actually frustration about dreams unfulfilled.

Pin-drop silence permeated the Colorado locker room. This was the most silent locker room I had ever been in. It was a time of self-reflection. So much of our collective emotion was invested in that game, only to lose and watch our former head coach walk out of our lives once again. We felt robbed. It was a long flight back to Boulder, and our team was going to have to pick up the pieces of dealing with still more disappointment surrounding Rick Neuheisel.

Our 1999 team finished the season with an absolutely disappointing record of 7-5. However, the highlight of our season was destroying Boston College, 62-28, in the Insight.com Bowl. Every facet of our capability, synergy as a team, and connection with Barnett as our coach was on point, finally. But it was the last game of the season. This was the way our team should have performed throughout the entire season. For most schools, a 7-5 season would have been a decent season. But it was a terrible season for the 1999 Buffaloes. Our team had not been focused since Rick Neuheisel left us, and it definitely showed on the field. For every talented athlete and every talented team, always remember, TALENT ONLY MEANS YOU HAVE THE CAPABILITY TO BE GREAT. Whether or not you are great, is something that has yet to be determined.

CHAPTER 26

Breaking Into the Lineup

AS I GROW older, I am constantly reminded of how things don't always happen when you want them to. Instead, timing is according to God's plan. I would have never anticipated waiting until my junior year to get my first true opportunity to break into the starting lineup. But that was my fate. I sat on the bench for two years behind two NFL draft picks. Both were exceptional college cornerbacks! However, I was still on track to accomplish all of my dreams and goals for my career. A player is always in prime position to go to the NFL when he plays for a well-respected college football program.

It was confirmed early in the off-season from coach Barnett, he loved Donald Strickland, and he was definitely going to be the starting cornerback on one side of the field. The other side was up for grabs! Donald and I worked our ass off that spring and summer. We knew the opportunity that was at hand. It was a fabulous opportunity for both of us to start for a major Division 1A football program, at the same exact time! We constantly pushed each other during workouts. All Donald and I ever talked about was what it was going to be like starting the season together, our very first game, against Colorado State.

Our schedule that year was ridiculous. We were actually ranked by many pre-season college magazines as #1 for the "toughest schedule." Our 2000 schedule consisted of games against USC, Washington, Texas, Texas A&M, Kansas State and the soon-to-be #1 ranked Nebraska Cornhuskers.

So looking at our schedule with the optimism and swagger I had at the time, I saw it was tailor made for anyone who wanted to make a name for himself in the world of college football.

Back in our hometown of San Francisco there was a major buzz about the Riordan boys. Who would have thought two kids from a small school in San Francisco would become the starting cornerback tandem for one of the more high profile college football teams in America? There were actually news reporters interviewing our old high school football coach, Kenny Peralta, about his prep stars that were now both starting for C.U. Our dads would boast on a daily basis at their jobs about their boys playing major college football. Our parents were planning to travel to games together once the season began.

Donald and I stayed in Boulder all summer running, lifting, and covering receivers as a part of our daily routine. It was during our summer conditioning program when Corey Chavous came to work out with us. At that time, he was a starting cornerback for the Arizona Cardinals, but now he is respected as one of the top NFL Draft Analyst. Many pro athletes came to Boulder to train because of the thin air and our great strength and conditioning coach. Anyone who knows Corey Chavous knows that he loves football and keeps a close eye on the players who play the game. I ended up taking a ride with Corey from our athletic center to our summer workout fields one day, and to my surprise, Corey had about four college football magazines on his back seat. As soon as I told Corey my name, he knew exactly who I was. He grabbed one of the magazines and shared his knowledge about my background. I was shocked that he really knew who I was. I had been watching him play on Sundays for the past two years, but Corey had been keeping his eye on the young, up-and-coming cornerbacks in the game too.

During our workout, I looked at it as my first test to see if I was the caliber of athlete who could compete in the NFL. Early on in the workout, I realized not only was I able to keep up with Corey, I was able to BEAT HIM! Now trust me, I didn't get too big-headed about the workout because I knew Corey was just beginning to get into shape for the upcoming season, and I had already been in shape. But it absolutely gave me the confidence I needed in my first summer training camp as the lead candidate to start alongside Donald.

The 2000 summer training camp was not only physical preparation, but a mental grounding as well. I knew I was going to be tested early and often. First I would be tested by our offense in practice, and if I managed to get through that test, I would be tested against our opponents during the season. The previous starting cornerback tandem, were both drafted and were very well respected cornerbacks in the Big XII Conference. With both gone, and now young, unproven cornerbacks replacing them, Donald and I counted on opponents coming our way early in the season to see if we were up for the challenge. It was our job to be ready for the challenge.

The opinion of our head coach, Gary Barnett, was that my best friend, Donald Strickland, was the best cornerback on our team. He felt that Donald's past performances in games and practices earned him a starting cornerback spot on our team. Interestingly enough, I was listed as the starting cornerback opposite Donald in every news publication throughout the country. But everyone within our team's inner circle pretty much knew I was the one player on our starting defense that Gary Barnett would not hesitate to yank. And subconsciously, I knew that I was not one of Gary Barnett's favorite players. However, I did not let this deter me. My father had always taught me to get myself in position with my production on the field so that a team cannot afford to put me on the bench. MY MISSION was to do just that!

Gary Barnett and I bumped heads often because of my flashy playing style. Barnett had a very blue collar, bring-your-lunchbox-to-work attitude and persona. My playing style and swagger was straight out of the Deion Sanders school-of-entertainment handbook. With every play in practice, or during a game, I made sure everyone realized it. That's how my playing style had been since Pop Warner Football (little league)— LOUD and FLASHY! I was not going to change my game just because I had a new coach.

Coach Vance Joseph, our team's assistant to defensive backs, pulled me aside one day to have a serious one-on-one. He informed me that a starting cornerback position had been dedicated to me for our first game against Colorado State. This came across as a warning when he added that I'd be on a very short leash with no room for error. We had a young, talented red-shirt freshman corner named Phil Jackson. Gary Barnett was just itching to see him perform in a game situation. Although Phil was no better than me, and sure as hell had not been with our program long enough to have paid the dues I had, IT STILL DIDN'T MATTER! I was not one of Gary Barnett's recruits. I was Neuheisel's recruit. The Gary Barnett/Terrence Wood relationship consisted of make plays, or ride the bench. The message was straight to the point, and my talk with Coach V.J. basically solidified what I already knew.

A great piece of advice I hand over to players now is how to change NEGATIVES *to* POSITIVES. I have spent well over half of my football career trying my best to prove people wrong. Some would agree that there has to be something that haunts you into becoming the best that you can possibly be. Jerry Rice came into the NFL being told he was too slow. This label troubled Jerry so much, that he worked hard to become faster and is arguably the best receiver that has ever lived! Michael Jordan was told that he was not good enough to make his high school basketball team his sophomore year. Mike used this as motivation to hone his talent into stronger skills, and likewise, he became the greatest basketball player in history. Rejection can accelerate one's drive, and thus his or her career. Greatness is available to those who dare to beat the odds. Or should I say to those who have the determination to beat the odds? I didn't want to be good; I wanted to be GREAT!

I ended up having a great summer camp and finished with the most interceptions by far, of any player on our defense, the summer of 2000. I felt good going into our season opener against the Colorado State Rams. I had my swagger back, and everyone could see it. The college football world was anxious to test the Colorado cornerback duo of Terrence Wood and Donald Strickland. And likewise, Donald and I were just as anxious to show the college football world that we were not to be tested!

CHAPTER **27**

Rocky Mountain Showdown

THE DAY WAS finally here! The day I would formally introduce myself to the college football world! When I woke up that morning I was excited as hell! But then all of a sudden I started getting really nervous. And then I got really excited all over again. I didn't know exactly how to feel about the BIG GAME. All I knew was that the two years I spent riding the bench and complaining about my playing time, were now over. Now it was time to PUT UP or SHUT UP!

Our 2000 season kicked off with the annual "Rocky Mountain Showdown" against Colorado State. My sophomore year, the game was so big that it was permanently moved to Mile High Stadium, which is now known as Sports Authority Field, home of the Denver Broncos. The stadium holds well over 70,000 people and is sold out every single year that the Colorado Buffaloes and Colorado State Rams bump heads. The game doesn't get much national coverage, but trust me, there are not many rivalries in college football that can guarantee over 70,000 people at the game, year after year.

I remember feeling sick from anxiety as I suited up for that opening game. I had secured the starting position, and now I had dreams to move forward with it. As soon as we broke down in the locker room as a defensive back unit and headed toward the field, a smile broke out on my face from behind the visor on my facemask. Today was going to be *my* day, and I could feel it. The animosity on the field between opposing teams as well as fans was thick. The year before, there had been many fights and arrests of unruly fans in the crowd. Colorado State was coming into the game with a very good team. They had won a Holiday Bowl championship the year before and they still had many great players returning.

Before the game, Donald and I gave each other a hug and some words of encouragement, using profanity that would not be appropriate for this book. As we ran out on the field with the starting defense, I noticed that the crowd had definitely filled in from the pregame warm-ups. Now the stadium was packed with 76,000 screaming fans wearing black and gold on our side, and green and gold on the other side. By now, I was damn near ready to piss in my pants. We broke the huddle and I ran out to my position. I couldn't believe it was really my time. No more wind sprints, no more weights, no more practice. We were on the air, LIVE! Now, it was me, against the opponent who didn't give a damn, whether it was my first start, whether my family was watching, or whether I was a nice guy, or not. His job was to beat me, and my job was to beat him. Only sixty minutes stood between the final outcome and us.

As the Colorado State offense lined up for their first play of the game, I fully anticipated them putting the ball in the air, but they elected to run the ball instead. My heart was about to beat out of my shoulder pads every time I lined up for the next play. The first half was pretty quiet on my side of the field, even though I was only getting half the snaps at the corner position, because Gary Barnett decided right before the game to make me split series with Nate Wright, my training camp competition. Our team went into the locker room at halftime with a 10-point lead.

We had a quick position and team meeting, and then we were back on the field for the second half of the game with a chance to close out the Colorado State Rams. As soon as we hit the field for the second half, Colorado State took to the air. It was the beginning of the 3rd quarter when they decided to test me.

I was covering a smaller fast receiver at the time, by the name of Dallas Davis. Anxious to make my presence felt in the game, I started thinking of a way to take a calculated gamble. I knew as I lined up against Davis, if they were going to take a deep shot, the ball was probably going to him. He exploded off the line of scrimmage, planted his foot, and cut in. I was sold on the fact that Davis was running a quick slant route, so I jumped it hard trying to get into the passing lane for the interception. As I closed down fast on the receiver, I noticed that he had made a quick cut up field and was actually going deep. Shit! I had guessed wrong and they got me on a slant and go! All I could do at that time was turn around, put my head down and pray that the quarterback overthrew the receiver or that the receiver dropped the ball. As I began to run after Dallas Davis, I knew the ball was in the air because as I gained ground on him, I could see his eyes tracking the ball with confidence. I knew there was no way for me to get close enough to break up the play, but I would be close enough to make the tackle after the catch.

Once I caught up to him after the catch, I actually let him gain another 4 yards because I was so caught up in the idea of trying to strip the ball from him that I forgot to tackle him. After we got off the ground, the first word out of my mouth was "Shit!" Years later, my mother shared with me that the same word came out of my father's mouth at the same exact time on that play, thousands of miles away in Northern California, as my family watched the game on TV.

My first real action of the game and I got hit up for a quick 35-yard gain. Colorado State fans went crazy. Their team was on our 15 yard line trying to punch the ball in courtesy of my big mishap. I couldn't help but glance to the sideline to see if I was going to be coming out of the game. There was no Nate Wright running onto the field, so I figured I still had time to make up for my mistake. On first down from the 15-yard line, Colorado State tried a run play right up the middle with no luck. On 2nd down, Colorado State tried passing the ball and ended up taking a sack. Now it was 3rd down and there was no way Colorado State wanted to settle for a field goal after getting so close to the end zone. Momentum swings are everything in football, and as such, Colorado State's coach figured they could take advantage of our free safety in coverage and throw a corner route to the slot receiver in the back of the end zone on my side of the field. Of course I didn't know I would catch my first interception at the collegiate level in that game.

As our defense lined up for the play, we knew that this would be a big play in the game. If we could keep Colorado State out of the end zone after they managed to get in the red zone, all the momentum would be ours. I personally had my mind on clearing my debts, and I was about to get my shot. I lined up on the right side of the defense in man coverage against a little quick receiver by the name of Pete Rebstock. Colorado State had sent a receiver across the formation my way right before the play started. As Rebstock came off the line of scrimmage, he only took two steps up the field and stopped. I knew they would not run a 2-yard route if they were really trying to score. I took a peek inside at the quarterback, who was totally intent on throwing the ball my way. He opened up ready to release. It was clear that he was not aiming for my man; instead he was going to the receiver who had come in motion right before the start of the play. The receiver had a step on our free safety Robbie Robinson and was heading for the back of the end zone, right behind my head. I bolted towards the back of the end zone! And as the ball was heading right into the Colorado State receiver's hands, I crossed in front of his face and stole the ball right out of the air. I took a quick look back at the Colorado State quarterback as if to say, "Gotcha back!" and then I took one knee to down the ball in the end zone. Touchback!

Our crowd went bananas! Not only had our defense not given up any points. We also got the ball back for our offense. I had just got my first collegiate pick on national television and redeemed myself from the big pass I had given up earlier on that drive. NOW IT WAS TIME TO BALL! We went to the sideline and I was getting love from all of my teammates. Our offense ended up getting a couple of 1st downs and then had to punt the ball away. Nate Wright, the cornerback who was sharing time with me in the game, had given up a couple of plays earlier in the game. So after my first interception, the coaches decided to keep me in the game.

The subsequent time our defense hit the field the Colorado State Rams must have felt that my first interception was a fluke. They decided to come right back at me the very next play with their speed receiver, Dallas Davis. I read the play from the very beginning. That's when the track meet began. Davis had his head down and was running deep down the field to a certain spot where he knew that ball was going to land. That's when I put my head down and began to put it into fourth gear. I knew I had to reach that spot on the field before the ball got there. I guess the Colorado State quarterback underestimated his own arm strength and the thin "mile high" air. He overthrew his receiver and I was able to adjust better to the ball and made a sensational diving interception about 50 yards down field. I actually used my body to cradle the ball as I hit the ground. When I lifted the ball in the air for everyone to see as I rolled over, the referee quickly awarded me with my second interception of the game. After that pick, Colorado State decided to leave me alone for the rest of the game. Now, the cornerback position opposite Donald was definitely mine, if anybody had any doubts.

Colorado State managed to come back and win the game by 4 points, which put a damper on my two-interception game. But, I managed to catch the attention of anyone interested in college football cornerbacks. My team's coaches, NFL scouts and my college football peers, got to catch a glimpse of what #23, Terrence Wood, was capable of. It may have taken me three years to get a chance to show my talents, but my world had instantly changed in less than four hours.

After the game, I called home immediately. As soon as my dad heard my voice he started going crazy. He said I had the whole city going crazy. Family and friends were ringing my parents' phone off the hook. Everyone was so proud. One of my dad's good friends, David White, who has trained numerous great players in the Bay Area, told my father that he was watching the game from a sports bar in Pacifica, a beach town about 12 miles outside of San Francisco. David said, when ESPN flashed on the screen that I lived in Pacifica, the bar went crazy! I was officially on the map. People on our campus and in my classes were complimenting me on a great game. Now people wanted to interview me and get ahold of my time.

Most significantly, I was finally getting some damn respect from our coaching staff. I was labeled a playmaker. I knew as long as I could hold onto that label I would attract the attention of the right people. Our next game was against Carson Palmer and the University of Southern California Trojans. My dream school!

It was the school where my grandfather became the first-ever, African

American quarterback in the Pac-10 (Now Pac-12). Yes, I repeat, *quarterback*. I had a big game against Colorado State but by no means did I have time to rest. We had to travel west to sunny Southern California. Although it was very early in the 2000 college football season, I was going back home to California as the interception leader in Division 1A college football. The game would take place at the Los Angeles Coliseum. Needless to say, being a California native, my entire family was trying to rearrange their schedules to make it to the game.

Since a Colorado versus USC game was a rare event at the time, the game was on ABC Saturday night prime time. Like I said, the layers of pressure do not let up when you are trying to reach the top. The layers only get added on! I wanted to be big, and I was fully aware of what could happen if I had a big game on a stage of this magnitude. I was determined to come back to Colorado with a win and still carry the title of being the country's interception leader. I would have to go through my childhood dream school in order to accomplish this huge goal. But when you're a man on a mission, does it really matter who is standing in your way?

CHAPTER 28

Tailspin

LOOKING BACK DURING this pivotal time in my college career, I would say that I was a little too cocky, with only one game as a starting player under my belt. There is a thin line between being confident and being cocky. The USC game was a quick, but stern lesson in the art of being humble.

The week before we played USC, I had a great week of practice and watched plenty of film on Carlson Palmer and the USC receivers. I went into the game feeling ready to remind everyone that last week was no fluke! I remember standing on the sideline at the Los Angeles Coliseum, watching the opening kickoff of the game, and feeling literally weak in my legs. It felt as though the mixture of playing on such a grand stage and playing against USC (my childhood dream team) had overwhelmed me. I had always dreamed of being on the home team sideline, but it was still amazing to actually be physically there, even if it was as an opponent. There was so much going on in my head. I knew my family was somewhere in the stands, but the Los Angeles Coliseum was so big that there was no way I was going to be able to spot them. That didn't stop me from scanning the crowd and wondering where they were. Each moment on the sideline increased my anxiety. The butterflies in my stomach were swarming. It wasn't until I was called into the game and collided with an opponent that my butterflies went away.

USC was running a form of the "west coast offense" at the time. This meant breaking into the game with numerous short passes. Donald and I were constantly getting routes that were thrown in front of us. No complaints on our end because as long as we made sure to wrap when making tackles, we'd be golden. However, this was something I failed to do.

I ended up missing a couple of tackles that I really should have made, which put our defense in a couple of tough situations. I still didn't feel confident enough in my relationship with coach Barnett to stop glancing over to the sidelines to see if I was coming out of the game. I had become consumed with whether or not I would get replaced, when I should have been claiming the starting position as mine whole-heartedly. Instead, I allowed fear to dominate me and cause me to underperform. I tensed up and played cautiously for the rest of the game. After a few missed tackles, I had lost my confidence because I did not know how to play the game without having the backing of my coach.

Always remember, when your job is on the line, it's best to relax and play the game as though the position will always be yours to keep. Don't be afraid to let your destiny take its course, whether you believe the odds will be in your favor or not. Every professional athlete can narrow his success to a few key defining moments in his or her career that contained the power to change his/her career forever! These key flashes in time are what I call defining moments. Like a Joe Montana pass to Dwight Clark in the back of the end zone, or Tom Brady's first Super Bowl after taking the reins to the Patriots from quarterback Drew Bledsoe. If athletes can learn to take advantage of those defining moments in their career, they can quickly find themselves on the fast track to accomplishing whatever it is they desire for their career. But unfortunately, many miss their windows of opportunity and by the laws of the universe, and the game we play, someone else must cash in.

One of my defining moments occurred in the 2nd quarter of the USC game. The Trojans were on our 10-yard line trying to punch the ball in on 3rd down and goal. As Carson Palmer and the Trojans approached the line of scrimmage, I recognized the offensive formation that they were lining up in. Every cornerback that has ever made a play in a big time game knows that instincts are key to being able to anticipate a play. After all the missed tackles earlier in the game, I was in desperate need of a big play. I knew that if USC decided to run the same play that I watched on film earlier in the week, my man would be the first option for Carlson Palmer to throw to. The team's location on the field revealed the fact that the receiver would be running a quick slant. I had already rehearsed this particular play in my head 100 times since I watched the USC offense operate on film earlier in the week. And every time I visualized that play, my visions always concluded with me taking an interception back for a touchdown! Given that the ball was in our red zone, a magical moment would have to occur. If I was going to make my vision come true, then I would probably have to score a 99-yard touchdown, which was fine by me.

At that moment the ball was snapped. I got the exact route I visualized earlier in the week. As the receiver planted his foot to cut towards the middle of the end zone, I cut him off and jumped in the passing lane. That's when I found out why Carlson Palmer won the Heisman Trophy, and at times has been considered an upper echelon NFL quarterback. He noticed that I had jumped his receiver's route and threw the ball to the backside shoulder of the receiver where only the receiver had a chance to make the play. The receiver did just that! It was a touchdown for the Trojans and the crowd went crazy as they began to strike up the band. As I picked myself up off the ground, I couldn't help but say to myself, "Damn it! You hesitated!" We tried to block the extra point. Then I had to take that long jog back to the sideline and look at our head coach who never even wanted me on the field in the first place.

Not long after the Trojan's touchdown pass, coach Barnett took the opportunity to make official what he wanted from the beginning of the season. Barnett told our linebackers coach, Kyle Cabral, to inform me that he was replacing me with a red-shirt freshman cornerback, Phil Jackson. It didn't matter how hard I had worked in the off season, It didn't matter if I was playing back home in California and my entire family was watching, and it damn sure didn't matter if I had made two interceptions for our defense in the game before. The USC game was going to be my last time starting in the 2000 season for the Colorado Buffaloes. I felt as though all the hard work and preparation for the season didn't mean anything. I was now reduced to a back-up role and was not even given the opportunity to finish the rest of the USC football game.

We ended up losing that game by three points. We had a chance to tie the game with a late field goal that was missed. I continued to play in the game as a nickel back, which is the team's third cornerback who usually comes in the game on passing downs. It's very similar to basketballs frequently played 6th man.

But truthfully my thoughts were not anywhere near the stadium. I felt overwhelmingly robbed and disrespected. When you hear you are on a short leash with a coach, it never really hits you until he pulls on that leash. Barnett had yanked the plug without even saying anything to me personally. Respect was certainly a courtesy that we lacked for each other. I found myself starting to second-guess myself. This was something I had never done before in my football career.

I watched my back-up finishing the game at my position as the sequence of possibilities played itself over and over in my head from the sideline: "If I make the interception and run it back for a touchdown... and..." I was still the country's leader in interceptions, but I was on the bench. The touchdown pass to my side was a play of astronomical proportions, and I was very aware that I missed a big time opportunity. Had I been in the moment, instead of out-of-my mind worried about whether I'd be called back to the sidelines, I could have risen to the occasion. Unfortunately, delusions of grandeur mixed with poor mental discipline clouded my judgment. This defining moment was a negative one that cost me the starting position.

After the game, I didn't even want to leave the locker room. We had roughly about 45 minutes to chat with friends and family depending on how long it took to get out of the locker room. I felt like I had made a bunch of mistakes that I would never get a chance to make up for. My family was waiting for me outside and the first thing my father said to me was, "Be prepared for the coach to try and officially replace you this week." My father shared the same thoughts as me, but they were by no means the first words that I wanted to hear coming out of his mouth after a disappointing game.

My mother and grandmother kissed and hugged me like they missed me and didn't want to let me go. I had been in need of that type of love for a while. After I caught up with my family, I hit the team bus. It was a quiet ride to the airport as the entire team reflected on the game and our performance as individuals, and as a collective unit.

On the plane ride back to the Denver airport, I couldn't help but wonder if I would get one more chance at starting; especially considering the fact that our next game was round two against our former coach, Rick Neuheisel. In my entire football career, I had never had two bad games in a row. In fact, after having a bad game, I usually followed up with a great game. All I needed to do was keep myself in the starting lineup long enough to remind everybody that the Colorado State game was no fluke, and I would be good.

Unfortunately, I didn't get that opportunity. We got home late Saturday night, rested Sunday, and by Monday I received a call to meet with my position coach, Tom McMahon, in his office before school. I knew right away something was up; coaches never call players early in the morning to meet face-to-face unscheduled, unless it's important. As soon as I hung up the phone, you know I had to get Big Vic's opinion about the emergency meeting. But at nine in the morning he didn't really lend the powerful insight that I was looking for. I threw on my jeans, Timberland boots, shirt, and jacket and headed out the door to go meet with my coach. I started trying to recall anything I had done over the past couple of months that could have got me in trouble. But I couldn't think of anything.

When I arrived at coach McMahon's office, he instructed me to sit down. On his desk there appeared to be what looked like a depth chart for our upcoming game against Neuheisel's Washington Huskies. Coach began to ask me how I thought I played in the USC game. I told him that I was not happy with my performance and I knew that I had to perform better. He shook his head in agreement and then paused. With slight apprehension, he informed me that the red-shirt freshman Phil Jackson would start at my position against Washington. I was shocked! He gave me the impression, however, that the decision was not his. He then tried to soften the blow by telling me that he was still going to keep me starting in our nickel and dime packages. Still in shock, his words started to fade.

I hung my head down as a million different things raced through my mind. I was pissed! I knew coach Barnett couldn't wait to replace me, but truthfully, I thought I would get more of an opportunity than I did. This was going to be a new experience for me. I had never lost my position before. I was accustomed to pursuing someone's job or having someone pursue mine, but never in life had I ever lost my position. Things had drastically changed. Some can adjust during times of adversity, while others really struggle. This meeting was another defining moment in my life and how I responded would determine the rest of my career at Colorado. I was not a freshman anymore and time was no longer a luxury!

CHAPTER 29

Hard Lesson Learned

WHEN FACED WITH adversity, a person always has two options: Either fight through it, or run from it. Losing my position changed my whole attitude towards football. The sport I loved was quickly becoming the sport I despised. Outlook has everything to do with results. If you despise your wife, your marriage will be terrible. If you despise your job, you will be a terrible employee and if you despise the sport you play, you can never become a great player. The worst part about my attitude is that I didn't care! I was exhausted with the politics of the game. Something that I never had to deal with earlier in my football career, now felt inescapable!

What I now realize after all of my years of playing football is that the politics are the other half of the game. Where there is big money, there will be big politics. Trust me! And in order for people to justify the big moves they make, they base it in the politics of the issue. It's one big cyclical relationship.

The secret loophole in this political tug of war is realizing that you are not powerless. If a player truly feels that he is getting the bad end of a coaching decision, then he must do everything in his power to change it. Complaining and sulking will only worsen your outcome. Instead of reacting, I should have had a pro-active attitude. I failed to realize that I truly possessed the power to get myself out of the situation I was in. Athletes who find themselves in highly competitive situations have to be able to find the inner strength to perform at a high level, even when they might not have the same opportunities as others. As hard as it may be to keep on smiling and work hard, it's exactly what you have to do! This is what truly speaks volumes about your character.

In my case, things quickly began to snowball in the WRONG direction. Everything was wrong about me! You could tell from my work ethic and attitude that football was not high on my priority list, after I was replaced. I found myself just going through the motions at practice instead of trying to get better. I had accepted defeat and given into it.

To all the young players out there, every day focus on improving yourself for you and no one else. Trust me, if you get better every day, your team will get a little better every day as well. I had mentally checked out of the University of Colorado football Program back in the 4th quarter of the USC game, and everyone around our football program could tell. I was part of the reason we didn't do so well that year.

Morale is everything, and one bad apple can spoil the bunch. Poor morale and poor work ethic are contagious. We had an extremely tough season that year, winning only four games. It was hard for me to grasp the concept of how my season started on national television with two interceptions, only for me to ride the bench behind a freshman in the end.

The worst part was that I didn't feel like I could pull myself out of my funk. I felt as though I had let my parents down. I truly believed that my welcome had run its course at the University of Colorado. It was no longer what I had signed up for, and I was officially ready to leave. I wanted to hang up my #23 jersey, my black and gold helmet, and part ways. All of my teammates knew I wanted out and actually supported my decision. I had one year of NCAA eligibility left and I desperately wanted to spend it as a starting cornerback on someone else's team. Due to NCAA rules, my only option with one year of eligibility left would be to transfer to a Division 1AA school. At the time, I was looking at a school named Saint Mary's in Moraga, California.

One evening, I called my father, like I did every week, and I absolutely lost it! I began sobbing, literally crying over the phone, telling my father that I wanted out. He knew I was serious because I was the type of kid who never complained. Even if I were unhappy with something I would always hold it in and suck it up. I never grew up sharing emotional moments with my father, but that night my dad sat back and listened to the pain of a son whose dreams seemed to be diminishing quickly.

I was convinced that the answer to my woes would be to transfer out and persuade my father for his approval. But to my dismay, my father was not on board. He said, "I know that you're hurting, and all of your feelings are totally valid... but you *started* at the University of Colorado and you will *finish* at the University of Colorado". This was not what I wanted to hear.

In my eyes, my father was forcing me to stay at this God-forsaken school. However, there is a little rule in my family that nothing gets started without getting finished. A rule I happened to be very familiar with. If you start a sport and you want to quit, then oh well! You don't have to play the following year, but you definitely have to finish something that has already been started. I couldn't believe I was thousands of miles away from my father, and officially out of his home, but his values and rules still applied. I hung up the phone that night with my father, prepared to never call him again. I figured that if I really wanted to leave I could market myself to a few different Division 1AA teams without him.

The next day I went into my position coach's office early. I had planned to tell coach McMahon that I was extremely unhappy and would no longer be with the team. As I walked into his office I could tell I had caught him off guard. He greeted me and then instructed me to take a seat. I told coach Mac how unhappy I was at C.U. and how I was thinking about exploring other options. I never officially said that I wanted to leave the program during that meeting, but little did I know that meeting would actually be the divine intervention that would keep me a Buffalo for my final year of eligibility.

Mid-rant, I noticed coach Mac disengage and stare out of the window as though he was contemplating something serious. As he turned back, he looked me dead in my eyes and said, "don't leave!" With great emotion he continued, "don't leave, T... you need to fight! I know that things have not turned out the way you anticipated, but you need to fight!"

I was totally caught off guard by coach Mac's show of emotion. He was usually a pretty tough and reserved dude, unless he was getting in your ass about a missed assignment. But watching coach tear up really halted my selfish rant. I think I just needed someone to show that they really cared about what I was going through. I left that meeting with coach Mac believing that if I left the University of Colorado, I would be letting him down.

That day I made the decision to suck it up and finish my commitment to the C.U. football program. I had absolutely no idea what would be in store for me during my senior year, but I could say that my talk with my position coach that day, opened my eyes to a few different things. The first thing was that I felt like I was the player that coach McMahon really wanted starting in his defensive backfield, but the decision was not primarily his call. Second, I had formed a bond with McMahon. Our relationship took more of a close personal turn for the better. What coach McMahon had mentored me in was something unrelated to the sport; it was intended to help me succeed in life.

Coach McMahon was no quitter himself. You see, he was riddled with health problems and persevered daily despite his condition. He didn't allow Type-2 Diabetes and daily insulin shots to excuse him from mentoring or achieving greatness. His passion for life and the game was insurmountable, even when he was diagnosed with lung cancer my senior year. He showed me that things don't always turn out the way that we expect them to. Only people of greatness are the ones who can fight through adversity. When the will is strong and the soul is energetic it's amazing what you can accomplish. So if you have found yourself in a rut—get up, dust yourself off, and go make things happen. Most importantly, remember that quitting is never an option!

CHAPTER 30

Do Or Die!

IT WAS THE summer of 2001 and I was fast-approaching the beginning of my senior football season at C.U. I had already spent four years at Colorado and it felt as though I had nothing to show for it. I had no individual awards, no championship rings, and no big BCS Bowl appearances. Not even the original head coach who recruited me was around.

Our entire graduating class wanted to take the bank in 2001! We all worked extremely hard those summer months leading up to our special season. We had just endured a terrible junior season, and we were anxious to erase it from our memories.

If I had one word to describe the mood of our team going into the 2001 season, that word would be <u>FOCUSED.</u> We were promised both Big XII Championship and National Championship achievements upon our arrival to Colorado by Rick Neuheisel. That's why we all chose to go to Colorado in the first place. But if our team was going to cash in on those dreams, it would have to be without Rick Neuheisel, and it needed to be now! There was no time left to say, "We can bounce back next year." Not when your NCAA eligibility is rounding the corner of its final lap.

For our team, the problem was not that we were not focused or hard workers. Our problem was that we were in a very talent-laden saturated conference at the time, known as the Big XII Conference. This is where Conference Championship trophies never come cheap, and they're always bundled up with a lot of hard work and sacrifice.

As for myself, I needed to make a move on someone's position if I was going to have any opportunity to touch my dreams of playing at the next level. Ironically for our team, as well as for me, the college football season of 2001 was "do or die." We all wanted to leave our mark on C.U. and many of us wanted to test our talents at the professional level, too. There was no way any of us would have anticipated just how special this season would be. What I learned during that magical season of 2001 was that all of the tests our team had been through in prior seasons were intended to groom us for a season none of us would ever forget!

Going into the season, we were estimated to finish in the middle of the Big XII, at best. What our opponents were unaware of is that when a team is destined to be a champion, there is no coaching, athletic talent, or politics that can stand in its way. Although coach Gary Barnett and I never had a great relationship, I give him large credit for helping our team visualize what we wanted to accomplish.

Coach Barnett first began to sell us on becoming Big XII champions during our team's winter conditioning program leading up to the 2001 season. A Big XII Championship was something that had not been talked about at Colorado since my red-shirt freshman year. In previous seasons, analysts had penciled in Texas or Oklahoma from the southern division, and Nebraska or Kansas State from the northern division to be the participants in the Big XII Championship game, and 2001 was no different.

The University of Colorado had lost pace with the arms race in the Big XII Conference. Our facilities, our talent, and our record for the past three seasons had all lagged behind the top-half of the conference. But we did have a large, talented senior class, and if we could muster up enough leadership to inspire the younger players, we figured we just might have what it takes to make our last game against Nebraska in late November actually count for something.

My college career had already been one hell of a rollercoaster ride by the time I approached my senior season. I had experienced the highest of highs, and the lowest of lows, both on and off the field by the time 2001 had rolled around. Little did I know, there were plenty more highs and lows rapidly coming my way! For some reason I could not get "do or die" out of my head during that time in my life. That would become my theme for the season. It was my mission statement.

Although I had been passed up for starting cornerback, I was smart enough to know that injury or poor performance could provide me another shot. The question was, whether or not I would be ready? Just like many of the other seniors on our team, I was quickly running out of time, the season was right around the corner, and it was time to find out what was in store.

CHAPTER 31

In Need of A Little Legal Help

THERE IS **NOTHING** part-time, or casual about success. If you have ever been around someone who is at the top of their profession, then I am certain you were able to identify his or her top priorities. What you will find is someone who is focused, knows what he wants and is determined to achieve it. If you had the chance to spend one off-season in the presence of Payton Manning or Tom Brady, you would understand very quickly why they are considered the best of the best.

I am actually ashamed at my lack of focus while I was supposedly chasing my dream during my college career. My mother once said to me, "Honey, we don't get what we want, and we don't even get what we need. We get what we deserve." Even though we may hate to admit it, many of us can look at our current circumstances, whether good or bad, and say I deserve my results. My peaks and valleys were no coincidence; they were a product of my effort. My problem in college was that I didn't know that becoming the *best* was a lifestyle! Becoming the best at your craft is not just something you can turn on and off. You have to live it. My off-the-field lifestyle began to cause friction with who I really wanted to become. I wanted to be great, but my actions were small. It was no wonder I hadn't secured the starting position.

The University of Colorado, just like the other major universities across the country, make sure there is always a lawyer within an arm's reach. Because whether it's a coaching staff who is being investigated by the NCAA on illegal recruiting allegations, or a young player who has been accused of being involved in a bar fight, big time programs make sure that they keep excellent lawyers on the payroll.

Lou Rubino was our team lawyer at the University of Colorado during my playing career. Lou was a constant figure around our program and he fought on behalf of many C.U. athletes in the past. Never once did I imagine that I would personally need his legal services. Nevertheless, my actions during my senior year dictated that I would become one of his defense cases.

One night while out partying with some of my teammates, I was pulled over on suspicion of drunk driving after leaving one of the local bars in downtown Boulder, Colorado. My heart quickly sank to the bottom of my stomach, but in the back of my mind, I figured that there was no possible way I would suffer any consequences. After all, I was a football player, right? I was convinced that once the cop walked up to my window and recognized my teammates and I, he would give us a break. Unfortunately, I couldn't have been more wrong.

When the cop approached the car, he proceeded to ask me if I knew why I had been summoned to stop. I replied, "no, officer." The police officer went on to say that I had made an illegal right-hand turn, and I had not turned into the nearest lane when I made my turn. I gave the officer a look of disgust, as if to say, "Are you kidding me? You pulled me over for that?" The next thing I knew, I was taking a Breathalyzer test, doing sobriety drills, then being handcuffed and stuffed in the back of his patrol car. As I sat in the back of that police car on my way to the county jail, I still had not really fathomed just how serious my situation was. I was in Buffalo territory, and I just knew that somehow I could slither and slide my way out of this situation. But I was wrong again!

After spending the night in jail, I was released and picked up by Big Vic. The local newspaper reporters had already sifted through the police reports from the weekend and spotted my name. By the time I got to our team's 6:30 a.m. winter conditioning practice that Monday morning, coach Gary Barnett was already well aware of my weekend mishap and requested for me to meet with him as soon as practice was over.

In coach Barnett's office, he asked to hear my side of the story, where I mentioned to him that I was barley over the legal limit, which had reduced my charges to a DWI (Driving While Intoxicated) instead of a full-blow DUI (Driving Under The Influence of Alcohol). I also threw in that I strongly believed that my traffic stop was racially motivated because of the pettiness of the crime. I wasn't swerving from lane to lane or speeding. I got pulled over because I went into the second lane instead of the nearest lane on a right hand turn. This was something sober drivers did all the time. Nevertheless, it was a traffic violation. When I was done justifying my actions, coach Barnett informed me that if I could get the charges against me dropped, I would not face any consequences. However, if for some reason the charges stuck, then I could be suspended for the first two games of my senior season. After leaving coach Barnett's office, I definitely felt that his ultimatum was fair and I was beginning to focus my efforts on getting my name cleared. I had worked too hard in conditioning camp and desperately did not want to have to sit out any games my senior year. That's when I made the call to Lou Rubino, for legal representation.

Given that I had no extra money to speak of, it was going to fall on my parents to take care of the fees. All day I pondered over how I was going to break the difficult news to my family. At the end of the night, I had not come up with a single plan. I decided to go over to my teammate's place to unwind. By the end of the night, my cell phone began to ring. It was my father. I remember thinking that the call was odd because my father is very much a creature of habit and he never called really early in the week, especially in the off-season. I answered the phone and this is when things got interesting. My father asked me if I was in a room where I could talk freely. I made my way into a private room and that's when my father unleashed his fury.

He began yelling and cursing about me getting arrested and the disappointment he felt because of the way he found out. I took for granted that my father, living back home in San Francisco, would have no way of knowing about my little mid-west transgressions. What I didn't take into account was that my father, a Channel 5 sports editor at the time, worked with people who had access to news wires that reported athletes who had been arrested in each state. Once I was booked into the county jail in Colorado, that information was available to the media outlets across the country to see.

My father's fire finally started to die down. He agreed that he and my mother would send the necessary funds to get a lawyer to represent my case. They were peeved that I had gotten myself into this situation, and even more outraged about having to pay for something they didn't do. But thank the Lord my family did have the means to help me fight my case. Otherwise, my senior year would have started with a 2-game suspension!

Eventually, I was cleared of all charges against me, and ended up pleading guilty to lesser charges. Coach Gary Barnett did indeed follow through with his word and I was never suspended for any games during my senior season. I didn't get away unscathed, that's for sure. I had embarrassed my family, the coaching staff, the University of Colorado, and myself. And my actions cost my parents a small fortune.

Off-the-field problems are the fastest way most players, both in college and in the NFL, find themselves in the doghouse. The biggest season of my life was staring me right in the face, and I was light years away from where I mentally needed to be. I knew that my senior year was going to be a season to remember. I just didn't believe it would get off to such a terrible start.

CHAPTER 32

Knocked Against the Ropes

AFTER ALL OF my legal issues, I was finally able to get my mind back into playing football again. Our team looked pretty good all throughout training camp and everyone knew and agreed on the expectations. All the college football analysts had considered our team out on the BIG XII Championship, but our team had a secret agenda that included playing in Dallas on December 1st for a BIG XII Championship trophy.

After a decent training camp, I still found myself second on the depth chart going into the season. One day in practice, I tore ligaments in my left thumb, which required me to go into the season with a cast on my left hand. However, I couldn't let the physical limitations cloud my vision and goals. Injuries are just a part of the game in the hard-hitting world of Big Time College and Professional Football. The team that hoists the championship trophy at the end of the season is the team that is able to endure through their injuries.

Our team was well aware that we needed to make a big splash on the college football scene early on, since we were not getting any respect in the pre-season publications. At the University of Colorado we had grown accustomed to starting our season against our intrastate rival, Colorado State. But when the opportunity was presented for our team to pick up a special early game at home, on national television, against Fresno State University, we did not hesitate to accept the challenge. Fresno State would be a great barometer to see exactly how good our team was, and simultaneously generate some attention from the rest of the schools around the country. The tricky thing about playing Fresno was that we knew you could not underestimate their team's ability because you would not only lose, you would also get hit right in the mouth.

Fresno State has one of those teams that never get's the credit they deserve, so they always play with a huge chip on their shoulder. Always! It was not going to be the first time our senior class lined up against the Fresno State Bulldogs. During our 1998 red-shirt freshman year, it took some very iffy home field calls by the referees and a late 4th quarter rally to keep us from suffering a very embarrassing home field loss. Needless to say, Fresno State was not going to come to Boulder, Colorado feeling intimidated by us. Conversely, they had a vendetta to avenge.

What our team did not know was that Fresno was coming to Boulder with one of the best teams they had ever had. Do names like David Carr and Brenard Berrian ring a bell? Due to my position on the current depth chart and the cast on my hand, my role was limited to only special teams.

I can remember that game like it was yesterday. It was a beautiful, warm, August night and the air just seemed right. We knew Fresno State would refuse to back down and we couldn't afford to either. This was going to be an all-out war! We battled each other through 2 quarters and there was no way to predict who'd win the game. By the halftime break, it became evident that if we were going to beat Fresno State, it was going to take all four quarters.

David Carr was looking every bit of the number one overall NFL draft pick that he would become eight months later. The Fresno State defense looked great as well, delivering some serious shots on some of our offensive players. Before we knew it, it was already the 4th quarter. Fresno State had managed to take a two-point lead with about 2 minutes remaining in the game, in front of a full-capacity Colorado crowd. Our backs were already against the ropes and this was just the first game of our so-called championship season. The game came down to the last minute and the last drive of the 4th quarter. If we were going to pull out this early season victory, it was going to take at least a 50 yard drive to get in decent field goal position!

As our team methodically moved down the field with our young soph-omore quarterback, Craig Ochs, it looked as if we were going to be able to survive the early season home field scare. Craig was highly sought after and known for his strong arm, and his moxy. There was plenty of reason to place hope on his shoulders! We were inside the Fresno State 15-yard line with about 43 seconds left on the clock, we elected to go for the touch-down, when our young season got rocked! Craig had rolled to his right looking for our most reliable receiver and team captain, John Minardi. He threw a fastball trying to pin the football right on John's #2 jersey in the back of the end zone. Unfortunately, Ochs didn't see the corner who was watching his eyes, and the Fresno State player baited him right into the game-clinching interception. Damn! A look of astonishment fell over the players, the coaches, and the entire crowd.

The Fresno State Bulldogs had stolen one from us at home, and had stolen all our aspirations of a championship and national respect. I felt robbed. I felt as though we had done all of our off-season work for noth-ing. After all our team had been through, you couldn't convince us that we weren't cursed!

However, it's amazing the blessings that can come your way after being knocked against the ropes. These blessings and lessons are only available to people and teams who are brave and strong enough to dust themselves off and get back up off the canvas. Although it didn't feel that way at the time, the loss to Fresno State ended up being good for our team. It brought us back down to reality and it forced us to support each other. People didn't expect much out of our team before the season and they defi-nitely didn't expect anything out of our team after the Fresno State loss. We were forced to look dead in the mirror and decide whether we wanted to complain and lay down, or get up and fight? And only time would tell which road we would choose.

CHAPTER 33

No Compromise

AFTER OUR TEAM'S opening-day loss to Fresno State, our team was absolutely devastated! We decided as a team to band together and fight. The seniors decided to take control of the team. It was necessary. We held a team meeting after our next practice. The meeting was not designed to be a discussion; it was strictly informational. All of the seniors informed the underclassmen that by no means were we going to compromise on the goal we sought to achieve at the beginning of the season. We set our sails out to be Big XII Champions and we were not going to anchor our ship until we accomplished our goal.

Respectfully speaking, championship teams are not led by a coach. A coach can ignite a flame in his team and guide his team, but eventually the players have to take ownership and continue to keep the flame burning. From that day on, The 2001 Colorado Buffaloes were on a mission! We worked harder than ever on the practice field and in the weight room. If there was anything good that came out of the Fresno State game it was having our ass kicked in the last minute, forcing humility on each and every one of us. We couldn't achieve greatness as an individual player, we had to band together and truly be a team. This was a defining moment for us as a group. We put our hard hats on and became dedicated to earn every single win from that moment on.

Our next game was against our cross-town rival, Colorado State, and unfortunately for them, they had to be the first team to pay for our team being pissed off! Colorado State got it handed to them in a humiliating thumping of 41-14. One by one, our opponents began to fall like dominos; we ripped off four impressive wins in a row before our big match up in Austin, Texas against the undefeated and eventual Big XII south champion, the Texas Longhorns. We began to climb up the college football rankings. A road win against a school of UT's caliber would open up some eyes around the country. But in order to fully understand the magnitude of the Texas game, it is essential to let you know about the twists and turns that led up to that particular event.

CHAPTER 34

The Ascension of Donald Strickland

ONCE OUR TEAM decided not to throw in the towel after the devastating loss to Fresno State, and decided to continue the course of becoming Big XII champions, it required many players on our team to take a long, hard, look in the mirror and pick up their game to an entirely new level. It also required many of us to stop talking about making big plays and start putting some action behind the talk.

As a result, one person's game began to blossom right in front of my eyes: my best friend and former high school teammate, Donald Strickland. My senior year, Donald's ascension to being recognized as one of the nation's top college cornerbacks, proved to be a very interesting scenario for the both of us.

Donald and I were more than just friends; we had become brothers. And often when family members and friends go after the same dreams, roles and relationships can change along the way. Our athletic careers were heading in two different directions, for reasons neither one of us could understand. Up to this point, because Donald was a year younger than I, he had always used my career as a barometer to see how his career was progressing. Now we found that our athletic relationship had drastically changed. Now, it was Donald who was a full-time starter and widely considered our team's best cornerback. I found myself sitting on the bench as a senior, watching someone I considered my younger brother become a star. To think that Donald had actually second-guessed coming to C.U.

because of the chance we might have to compete against each other for the same position, had been laughable in the beginning. Irony became reality. Donald was living proof that there is always someone hungrier, more dedicated, and more focused than you. And when you slack off, he will be there, putting in the work to pass you up. My complacency, my "T Wood" complex, and my bad attitude, all blew the door wide open for someone to pass me up. And it just happened to be my best friend.

This was a serious wake up call for me. Early in our careers, throughout high school and our first couple of years in college, Donald was the one who was always trying to keep up with me. He tried to keep up run-running sprints, defensive back drills, and in our team's stat books. But somewhere between the end of my junior season and the summer training program before my senior season, I found myself trying to keep up with *him*. His hard work earned him the faith of our coaching staff, and they did everything in their power to promote him. There was no denying that this kid was about to explode.

I also developed my own athletic momentum at the same time as Donald. Unfortunately for me, I hadn't quite realized that my off-the-field activities tested the faith of the coaching staff, and lead to me being viewed as second best. Momentum is one of the strongest factors that can be used for a player's benefit or demise. Often times, the smart players who are able to capitalize on positive momentum can find themselves riding that wave all the way to a very long and lucrative football career. But players riding the wave of negative momentum end up seeing their career going downhill quickly, wondering why they can never catch a break. I was clearly the player in the negative scenario. While Donald's career was taking off like a rocket, my career was quickly hemorrhaging. The worst part about it was that I had no idea how to stop the bleeding.

It was during our team's bounce-back game against Colorado State when I really realized that Donald was on his way to accomplishing his dreams. I knew that I was not going to see any playing time myself, so I made it a point to really watch Donald's game and ask him questions and give him pointers when he came to the sidelines. It was a way for

Donald to get feedback on his game, as well as a way to keep my mind in the game, in case I did somehow receive a chance to play. Our team had a strong hold on this game by the time we went into the locker room for half time.

It was a moment in the 3rd quarter that would bust the game wide open. As Colorado State came to the line of scrimmage, Donald lined up over the slot receiver on the right hand side of the defense. The ball was snapped, Donald dropped back into his zone, which indicated that our team was playing zone defense. This allowed Donald to look into the backfield and get a good read on the Colorado State quarterback's eyes staring down his receiver on a quick slant.

With explosive velocity, Donald broke on the ball just as Colorado State's quarterback was ready to release the ball. The play couldn't have been more perfect from my vantage point on the sidelines. It was so fluid that it seemed to go down in slow motion. Donald had a perfect read on the Colorado State quarterback, and cashed the check! Everything that followed was equally, textbook, as he proceeded to clear a touchdown after his first career interception.

Big-time athletes always have a strong drive to succeed, which always leaves them hungry for more! Once Donald got his first interception and the touchdown to follow, he became fervent for the next one. From that day on, Donald worked his fingers to the bone to ensure that a multitude of opportunities would transpire to achieve that feeling again.

You may be asking yourself, "What feeling is *that*?" Well, it's the feeling that most will never have the opportunity to experience. It's that unique feeling of having thousands of people watching you through eyes of worship. There is nothing equivalent to the "high" a performer feels when he is on a big stage and he is at the top of his game. And Donald was eating it up!

The next hurdle on the road to the Championship was against the San Jose State Spartans. This would be one of the two times that we would face San Jose State in a three-year period. It was always special for Donald and me to play against San Jose State considering we grew up only forty minutes away from the school. We personally knew many of the players and coaches on the San Jose State team. This definitely added more incentive for Donald and me to perform well.

Once again, I started the game in the same position, not knowing whether I was going to get any playing time or not. But in Donald's case, he was about to make another big play for the second week in a row that would grab the attention of not only all the Colorado Buffalo fans, but the-attention of all of the Colorado media as well. Early in the 2nd quarter, the San Jose State offense was backed up inside their own 5-yard line. Donald was over the slot receiver for San Jose State when their quarterback took the snap and began to roll out towards him.

The pressure from our defensive line began quickly bearing down on the opposing quarterback. He desperately needed to get rid of the ball or else he was going to get sacked in the end zone for a safety. Just as our defensive lineman was getting close enough to grab the San Jose State quarterback, the quarterback threw the ball towards one of his running backs that was trying to sneak out of the backfield. Like clockwork, Donald broke perfectly on the ball. He tipped it in the air as the running back fell to the ground. In that same motion, Donald jumped up and snatched the tipped ball out of the air and took about four steps before diving into the end zone. The crowd went crazy!

Donald's achievements grabbed the attention of the local news stations and even NFL scouts. A special news segment on Donald becoming the first defensive player in Colorado football history to score touchdowns in consecutive weeks was the highlight of the evening news. Within two weeks, Donald's stock had risen from an unknown college cornerback, to a young SUPERSTAR in the making.

I sat on the bench for the first portion of my senior season with Donald's ascension as the only source of pride I had left during some of my darkest hours. While many good friends would have separated through the journey of chasing the same dream, we grew closer and stronger. With every personal loss I had to endure, I found myself rooting even harder for Donald to win. We went from being good friends in high school, to becoming brothers in college. Dealing with the shifts in our athletic careers, I desperately needed a friend close by, a brother that would encourage me when no one else could, and someone who would believe in me when no one else would. This was a time to quietly reflect, to rededicate myself to the game both on and off the field. It was a necessary fall from grace; sometimes the lowest point is the only way to get focused again on the higher points!

CHAPTER 35

Blessing Others While Waiting For Yours!

ONE THING RARELY discussed between athletes, but is inevitable for most, is how to deal with waiting for personal success, while watching others achieve theirs. As I stated earlier, things don't always happen in our timing. Many times we have to be groomed for opportunities before they are presented to us, or they will be quickly squandered. But the task of waiting can be a source of major stress for high-octane athletes who have never had to wait for anything in their lives. You may be a hot young tailback waiting to get your shot behind a decent senior tailback. Or you may be a starting receiver, who's never the first option on any of your team's passing plays. Whatever the case may be, there are thousands of kids, on every level of football across America, who can't wait until it's their time.

It's cliché, but remember that Rome wasn't built in one day. All great things and all great people are developed over time. Everything from computer software to society is constantly under pressure to change for the better. People are no different. If you have to be second fiddle to someone else, don't spend your time envying that person. Accept the challenge of waiting as an opportunity to perfect your craft. Be "patiently impatient!" Study that person with every intention of incorporating what he does well, into your own unique package of skills. If you waste your time filled with jealousy, then you've also wasted your time to get better. Hatred never pays the bills; it only piles them higher. Patience is a virtue that I learned during my time on the bench. Giving someone the praise they deserve enriches your ability to be a team player, and creates opportunity for you. My simple advice to you is to be constructive and positive in your down time.

Keep in mind that when you finally make it, the rule is still the same. Now someone will be chasing you!

CHAPTER 36

Seizing Opportunity

EVERY COMPETITIVE ATHLETE prays and wishes for the right opportunities to come their way. Most do not realize how precious some opportunities are; other athletes are not even present enough to realize when real opportunities are staring them right in the face. Special opportunities don't present themselves every day, so it's important that you are aware and ready to seize them when they do.

I am blessed that I have had a handful of these opportunities in my life. Unfortunately, I was not prepared and ready to capitalize on all of them. But I have always kept my head up in anticipation of future opportunities coming my way. It's absolutely essential that aspiring athletes in both college and professional football prepare to capitalize on the opportunities they receive. The nature of the game is so competitive that really good opportunities are far and few between. Most people in any competitive industry get one shot, if they even get one shot at all.

The more time I spent riding the bench the first half of my senior season, the more dismal my dream of playing in the NFL became. Many of my teammates were receiving plenty of attention from NFL personnel and draft analysts, while I seemed to disappear from their view. I started preparing myself to give up on my dream of playing in the NFL. I just didn't see any hope at the end of the tunnel. I thought I'd be stuck in this hell-hole slot of riding the bench forever. I was convinced there was no playing time in sight for me. This was a very dangerous time for me.

I had stopped working on the practice field; I stopped listening to the coaches. I really didn't care about the outcome because I figured, "What's the point in working hard, if I will never get to reap any of the rewards?" This was the worst possible attitude to take. Luckily for me, the demanding physical nature of the game saved me.

The simple truth about the game of football is that every backup player is one play away from being a starter. Whether it is due to injury or lack of performance, many football teams spend a lot of time during the season shuffling guys in and out of certain positions. After sitting on the bench for the first three games of the season, I finally got my foot in the door when one of our cornerbacks didn't have his best game against the University of Kansas. I had a sweet game on special teams that day, so I figured our coach would decide to give me a shot as the team's nickel back position for the next game against Kansas State.

Kansas State was the #12-ranked team in the country. We had history with this team and by no means was the hostile environment going to make the task at hand any easier for our team. The matchup against Kansas was a tough physical battle for four quarters. Thanks to a surprisingly stingy defensive game and great special teams play, we were able to go into Kansas State's house and pull out a close 16-6 win. The locker room was rocking after the game because everyone knew that we had just got past a huge hurdle for our team. Our big win against Kansas State was my first real shot at some legitimate playing time in a long time. An unwritten rule in football is that no one gets demoted when you play decently in a big win. So in my mind, I anticipated at least maintaining the same amount of playing time, if not more, in the next game. It was all smiles as we boarded our team plane back to Boulder, Colorado. We could enjoy the win for a good 24 hours.

There was never really any down time on the road to becoming Big XII Champions. The next opponent on our team's championship mission was the Texas A&M Aggies, who flaunted a 5-0 record when they arrived at our home stadium. After the big win over Kansas State, it seemed as if the pace of the season began to dramatically speed up and every game we prepared to play held more weight and more expectations than the week before. Our team was now on the college football radar and with a win over the undefeated Aggies, people just might start to take the Colorado Buffaloes seriously. Our team was determined to gain respect! And if Texas A&M was who we had to go through to receive that respect, then line 'em up!

CHAPTER 37

Guess Who's Back?

I WOKE UP in the Omni Hotel the morning of the Texas A&M game, not knowing exactly what role I was going to play in the game later that afternoon. I assumed it would consist of playing only sparingly in a reserve role. I had talked with my father on the phone the night before the game I believe it was my father's way of feeling a part of my football career from a distance. My father had always been so influential in my football career while I was playing in high school, but once I picked up my luggage and headed off to play in Colorado, our relationship began to suffer from the separation. That night over the phone, I let my father know that I was not sure about the amount of playing time I was going to receive, but that I did have a great week of practice. This was a blatant lie. My focus during the week was everywhere but football. If I was going to accomplish anything on game day, it was going to be accomplished with pure talent and luck. My preparation, work ethic, and desire for football had left the building a long time ago.

I was playing decently, but when I felt like I wouldn't get any substantial due, I stopped putting in the extra effort. As I left the locker room to run out on the field that day, nothing felt any different than any other game. Half time flew by and the 3rd quarter began with an injury to one of our starting cornerbacks, Roderick Snead. I didn't stress over it because I wasn't our team's next option. The next option was Phil Jackson, a sophomore, who was less than impressive. I guess Phil was just as unprepared for this game as I was. The next thing I know, our defensive coordinator taps me on the shoulder signaling me to go into the game with the base (starting) defense.

Wouldn't you know it? When I least expected it, a crack in the door finally opened after years of me pounding on it, to no avail. If only I had not fallen into hopelessness, I would have been prepared for the opportunity! For some unknown reason, I happened to skim through a little film on Texas A&M earlier in the week. Maybe it was for the simple fact that they were undefeated at the time. I must have wanted to see what the fuss was all about.

As I ran onto the field, all I could think about was the horrible game I had against Texas A&M in my junior year. I decided to turn this negative experience into a little redemptive justice. From past experience, I knew that as soon as I stepped on the field they were going to start throwing the ball my way. But that didn't bother me at all. I think I had finally let go! I didn't care whether or not my head coach really wanted me out there or not. I was out there now and I planned on making it count.

I believe the first couple of times Texas A&M threw the ball my way they got a couple of short gains. After a while, I guess Texas A&M figured they had broken me in enough to try and go over the top with a deep route. Our defensive coordinator called a cover-3 defense then. A defense geared to halt any deep attempts. In cover-3, the main priority of a cornerback would be the deep 3rd on his particular side of the field. So when the Texas A&M receiver shot off the line of scrimmage, to try and get behind me, I was able to stay on top of his every move, given I had already anticipated that he'd take a deep route.

The one thing I didn't expect was for their quarterback to still try and throw the ball my way, with his receiver completely covered. My legs flew down the field. I remained stride-for-stride with the Texas A&M receiver while looking back at the quarterback launching the ball to wing it deep down my sideline. I knew the Texas A&M's quarterback saw that I had perfect coverage on his receiver, but he was bent on showing me up. His decision to throw the ball regardless of my position was a blatant show of disrespect for my skills as a cornerback. For this he would pay. It was Showtime!

The quarterback had gotten off a good, high pass, but it had hung in the air about 50-yards down the field, which caused the receiver and me to throttle down. We were both gearing down to prepare ourselves to jump for the ball. Defensive backs and wide receivers are all taught from a very young age that when there is a ball up for grabs, whoever can time his jump to catch the ball at its highest touchable point would win the catch. It became evident that my opponent had received the same training as I had. Suddenly, when the ball descended towards us, he exploded off the ground as if he was trying to pose for a *Sports Illustrated* cover photo.

As the Texas A&M receiver started to come down with the ball, I jumped in the air, and mid-leap, before we both fell hard to the ground, I ripped the ball right out of his hands! The way we fell made it hard to decipher if I had actually intercepted the pass or not. However, when I got up from the playing field, holding the ball high in the air, there was no question about it. The crowd went absolutely crazy! It was the interception of the year for our team and it came from someone who had been completely forgotten as a viable cornerback option.

In that moment, a wave of confidence came over me. It was as if I had risen from the dead. I went on to finish the game with 6 tackles, 2 tackles for loss, and added a second interception in the 4th quarter with a little less than two minutes left in the game. The best part about the day was the fact that our team won another big-time game. This meant that our Big XII Championship aspirations were one step closer to becoming reality.

It's amazing how fast things can change over night. Before the game, a reporter could care less about getting an interview with me. After the game, I had six different interview requests that I happily obliged. The bandwagon of coaches, trainers, and medical staff all began to show a shift in their behavior towards me. It had turned out to be a magnificent day! And the crazy thing is, it was totally unexpected. To go from being inconsequential to the probable Big XII defensive player of the week, in one day, was exhilarating! The honor was actually given to a fellow teammate who had an amazing game as well, but as a consolation prize, I was named our teams' Defensive Player of the Week. By pulling out a tough win against Texas A&M, our team finally managed to get a little notoriety within our conference. The undefeated Texas Longhorns were our next challenge. At the beginning of the season, they were favored by many to not only win the Big XII Championship, but possibly also win the National Championship. With little time to prepare before our next big test in Austin, Texas, our coaches had to make a tough decision about who was going to start at the cornerback position opposite Donald in this monumental game.

Even though I was not Gary Barnett's first choice, no one could ignore the game that I just had. I became tied for the team lead in interceptions in a matter of hours. And now the question on everyone's mind was, "Why isn't Terrence Wood starting?"

CHAPTER 38

The Blessing and Curse of an Alter-Ego!

ACCORDING TO SIGMUND Freud's Structural Model, "Your ego is the part of your individual self that has been modified by the direct influence of the external world." It's your conscious personality that directly controls your behavior. In my opinion, no one in the entertainment industry with substantial status has gotten there without an ego. Some call it cocky, some call it a swagger and some refer to it as having "it." Regardless of what you call it, you better have it, if you want to be big. For every person who will praise your every move, there will be just as many people tearing you down. Life is a balancing act in every aspect, and how you manage a healthy ego makes all the difference.

This is something that can actually prove to be extremely dangerous for many athletes because highly talented athletes have a very unique influence with the external world. It's not a secret that the most talented and proven athletes get their butts kissed. Extremely talented people in every field, will experience the same. So as a young athlete becomes more aware and conscious of the way he or she is favored by society, the athlete's ego can quickly begin to take shape. Egos are strengthened by reinforcement; that's the reason talented athletes will have some of the biggest egos you will ever come across. Now don't forget what I said in the very first paragraph: an ego is essential for success. But be aware that many have allowed their egos to compromise their success.

As an athlete matures in the ranks of his respective sport, he will often end up forming an alter ego. Entertainer extraordinaire Beyoncé Knowles went as far as naming her alter ego, "Sasha Fierce". People pay big money to see alter egos perform. A LeBron James fanatic may have his poster, jersey, bobble head doll, and autographed shoes. But that doesn't mean that the fan really knows LeBron James.

Sometimes, athletes are given nicknames by their peers, which actually begin the formation of their alter ego. In my case, my own nickname, "T Wood," was given to me at a very young age. And as my football career began to take flight, everyone around me began to refer to me as "T Wood." My teammates, my coaches, the media, and many other people throughout my life knew me exclusively as "T Wood." But never once in my life has my mother referred to me as "T Wood." To my mother, I was Terry, or one of a handful of other nicknames that I care not to embarrass myself by using within this book.

"T Wood" quickly began to become the *other* me, while the subdued "Terry" was the ordinary kid who went home to his family after every game. It can actually benefit an athlete's career to differentiate between the true self and his alter ego. Why? Because an alter ego can allow one to deal with the glitz and glamour of one's career, while the most important people in a person's life get to experience the true person.

I recently heard a well-known comedian make a joke about how he loves being on stage and in the public eye because he is greeted and treated with so much love and respect, as opposed to when he goes home to his wife and kids and is greeted with dirty diapers and chores. This is the perfect analogy of how we are all indeed two different people inside. One side of this comedian is a big time, famous comedian and television star, while the other side of him is just a regular husband and father. This is how the ego and alter ego can work in perfect harmony.

Trouble begins when the lines blur and the alter ego takes over the true person. Better said, it's when your alter ego becomes so over-bearing that you forget who the hell you really are. The spotlight they are in, the way they are treated by the public, and the stage that they perform on becomes so addictive that it gets extremely hard to turn off. This is when the off-the-field troubles arise because the alter ego is out of control. This is the

Dr. Jekyll/Mr. Hyde syndrome that can completely ruin the opportunity and life of a celebrity. The throwing of money in clubs, the promiscuous lifestyles, the drug use, and the thousands of dollars wasted on gaudy jewelry are all signs of a person who cannot control his ego. It's the need to get attention and feel respected once they are off the playing field that oftentimes causes them to go overboard with erratic behavior and flashy purchases.

Warren Buffet is one of the wealthiest people in the world. He is wealthy in temperament and wisdom, and is arguably our country's greatest investor. He has also added philanthropist to his title, giving away more than half of his $47 billion fortune to worthy charities through the Bill and Melinda Gates Foundation. If anyone has an excuse to have an over-the-top ego, or unabashedly throw money around in a club, it's Warren Buffet. But you'll never see a picture of Warren Buffet wearing a $100,000 diamond chain and platinum fronts, hanging out the side of a pimped-out Cadillac with a stripper on his lap. That would be laughable, and it should be no different for you or me.

There were times when "T Wood" began to control most of the decisions and thoughts for Terrence Wood, and I admit that the outcome was very rarely positive. At one point, my lifestyle was extremely fast: I was messing around with the wrong women, abusing drugs and alcohol, and being arrested on drunk driving charges; all of which was a product of the true me being over-taken by "T Wood." The more I indulged in my alter ego, the less I knew who the real Terrence Wood was anymore. I found that Terrence craved to be "T Wood" at all times. There was no longer the trademark separation between the athlete and the humble man that sustains greatness. My on and off-the-field lives became intertwined. Terrence always got respect, but "T Wood" was coveted. And believe me that was a BIG difference.

Someone may ask how does a big-time athlete keep his ego in check? The answer is as simple as being surrounded by people who can keep them grounded. This helps to ensure that the athlete's ego is never "still in uniform" when he is off the field.

Another distinction that separates a good athlete from a great one is having someone as a cornerstone. Whether you believe it or not, every great athlete has someone in his life that can push him to places that he never thought he could go. Great athletes crave to have someone around them who can get that last bench press rep out of them, or that last wind sprint, or that last sit up.

For me that was my father. He was the only person who was never afraid to let me know that I could work harder, or be better. He was the one that always pushed me to prove him wrong. I had developed a very strong ego about my football talents at a very young age, but my father always made sure that my ego could be brought back down to reality if need be. When you are really good at something at a very young age, but you still have someone who relentlessly pushes you to be better, that's called a blessing. Show me the athlete who can have swagger, but at the same time control it, and I will show you a person who will succeed in anything he chooses in life.

Have you ever saw a really pretty girl who was self-aware enough and nice enough to be humble about her beauty? The interesting thing is that she actually becomes even more beautiful, and finds herself adored by both women and men. Learn how to control your ego through humility and you will unlock the secret to being well-embraced and respected in all endeavors. You'll find people will do anything they can to help you, or be a part of your team once you've mastered this balance. A seamless life is the reward for talented athletes who learn and embrace humility.

Every single college football season, I get a kick out of watching the Heisman Trophy Award ceremony. Again, the Heisman is the award dedicated to college football's best player. Every year the top four players in the country are sent to New York for the award ceremony. Each year I've watched the ceremony, every invited player has displayed a great sense of humility and respect for the event honoring his achievements. Never once have I heard a player say, "I'm the best one here and I would be shocked if I didn't win this award." Even though every single player at the Heisman Trophy Award ceremony is *thinking* something of that nature, he would never say it out loud! It's not politically correct or good sportsmanship.

A Heisman candidate is no ordinary athlete. He is someone who has been very talented from a very young age. He's also someone who is very confident and fully aware of his ego, but knows the right thing to do. These athletes are worth millions because they know the right way to be portrayed in the public eye, regardless of how cocky they may truly feel on the inside.

Controlling the ego is an essential tool for young players to master. There is no bigger monster than the game itself. When you think that *you* are the franchise and you start to believe it, then you are forcing yourself into your own demise. Whether it's a six-figure college scholarship or a multi-million-dollar NFL contract, if a coach or general manager gets the sense that a player's ego is too big for his britches, heads will roll. Keep your head off the chopping block by developing smart business practices and etiquette *Before You Go Pro*. Know when to turn your shine down, and your humility up. Your ego is only as strong as the leash you have it on. The question is, will your ego be a blessing or a curse?

CHAPTER 39

The Short End of the Longhorns

EVERY COLLEGE FOOTBALL program in the country has had its highs and lows. There are only a handful of college football programs that can garner the type of respect a program like the University of Texas demands. It was hard enough to win a road game playing in the Big XII Conference, and it would be extremely difficult to go play in front of over 80,000 rowdy die-hard Longhorn fans. Having won the previous week against their intrastate rivals, Texas A&M, we knew there'd be no sneaking up on the Texas Longhorns. The Texas A&M game was a monumental win for us and we aspired to claim the same against the Longhorns as well.

There was no extended celebration after our victory over A&M. Just 24 hours later we were back in the facility preparing for the next do-or-die contest. Sore, banged up and fatigued, we were right back in the routine of our football discipline. Our training involved watching playbacks of our previous game against Texas A&M, along with light wind sprints to work out any soreness in our muscles. We all split up into our position meeting rooms to watch film. Donald and I sat right next to each other in the back row. As coach gathered all of his notes and got the video equipment situated, an uncomfortable silence filled the room because everyone knew someone was about to get promoted at the expense of someone else's loss. After all of the press I received for my good performance against Texas A&M, the team figured that when coach McMahon flashed up our depth chart for the week, Terrence Wood would finally be back in the starting lineup opposite his good friend Donald Strickland.

Finally, coach was settled with his notes, and shut off the lights. The teleprompter lit up, and he said, "Okay, here's the depth chart for our practice tomorrow in preparation for the Texas Longhorns." Although I had become humble about my playing time and football as a whole, my heart started beating as though I had just been running sprints at the combine. This was proof that there was still an ounce of passion and competitive juice left in me. As I looked up to view the depth chart, I couldn't believe my eyes; I had not moved one bit! I was still second string. This was the biggest disappointment of my career, yet. I hung my head low but remained casual. All eyes were on me as the entire defensive back squad took a quick peek back at me to gauge how I was dealing with the letdown. I was mentally finished!

Coach started the film to prep us for the game, as Donald leaned over and whispered, "Don't trip!" Donald knew, just like the rest of the defensive backs knew, that the job should have been mine. Instead, they decided to go back with Rod Sneed because he had recovered well from his injury, and I just wasn't the "flavor" coach Barnett preferred.

That week at practice was one of my worst ever at Colorado. Truthfully, if it weren't for the athletic department paying for my education and housing, I wouldn't have even shown up. I knew that I'd have some playing time in the game, but once again, I didn't know how much.

"How could they not start me after my stellar performances?" I thought to myself. I figured I would resign to doing the bare minimum; I just did whatever I had to do to survive the practice week. I felt like a fraud, going through the motions with little effect. I had become that guy that no one wants to be as an athlete. My love of football was fading with every week that went by on the schedule. I was consumed only with myself at that time in my life; and I regret that I dealt with my situation in this manner.

We left early Friday morning for the game. Going to class had been an afterthought for about 90% of our team that week. It's hard to concentrate on schoolwork when you're about to play in a game that has major B.C.S. Championship implications. Our professors knew the deal as they marked us absent for that day's class attendance. It's no secret among the staff that football players earn their "keep" by wearing cleats. The University of Colorado looked the other way in hopes that we would go out there and earn every red cent of our scholarship monies on the Longhorn field. And, it's no coincidence that colleges see student applications increase whenever its team wins a National Championship.

I took my seat on the plane and prepared for takeoff with the rest of the seniors seated at the front of the plane. As our assistant defensive backs coach, Vance Joseph, maneuvered his way down the aisle with his luggage, he leaned over and said to me, "Boy, if you ball in this game, you're going to make some money for yourself!" and walked off casually. If there was inside scoop to be had, I could always count on coach V.J. to shoot it to me straight.

If I were wise, I would have gravitated towards coach V.J. during those days. It's a shame that my thinking hadn't become so strategic yet. But I did know that coach V.J. knew something, and my assumption was that some of the NFL representatives, who may have been at our Texas A&M game or viewed the film of the game, must have inquired about me.

Unfortunately for me, I was still so bitter over not being first on the depth chart that I did not process coach V.J.'s message as an opportunity. I should have realized that with a strong showing, it would not matter whether or not I started anyway. Every week the games had become more intense, which meant that there would be more media exposure. If I had an explosive game, then this would be the perfect calling card to garner the attention of the NFL. My situation as the underdog was so perfect at the time, but I was too stubborn and disenchanted to recognize it as such.

For this reason, I warn you not to resign yourself to hopelessness because your curse and blessing may present themselves at the same time. Don't allow your pride, or resentment for others, to pierce your focus on your goals. For without focus, or a game plan, you will not get very far. It was no surprise that I had been handed the "short end" of the Longhorns. I let my resentment for our coaching staff pierce my focus, and an athlete who is not focused, is an athlete who will not get far!

CHAPTER 40

Longhorn Country

SURPRISINGLY WE WERE greeted by a swarm of well-wishers and supporters at the team hotel in Austin, Texas. But I was most concerned about one person in particular, one Delisa Jones. An amazingly beautiful young lady who had absolutely become the focus of my time and attention; she was my life, off the field. Delisa was the best thing going on in my life at the time, a pleasant get-away from the stress of the football program. It was quite a challenge to squeeze in some one-on-one time with her, given our team's tight schedule with meetings, films, dinner, and a looming curfew. Further complicating the task were the coaches' explicit instructions that we keep things short and sweet with family and friends until after the game. Of course, with my new found love for Delisa, I dedicated every last minute of time I could, to be with her before our team's mandatory bed check.

What I failed to realize was that I was not in good enough standing with our coaching staff to take a leisurely approach to our team itinerary the night before our biggest game. There was no time before the game that the coaches felt was yours to squander. Those who not only succeed, but also have longevity at the collegiate and professional levels of football, are those who transcend mere talent and become business-minded about their game. This is what we footballers refer to as the "total package".

Yes, I had a fabulous game against Texas A&M, but that was *last* week. I couldn't get away with anything now given that I wasn't first string in terms of attitude or team placement. But this did not stop me from stealing away extra minutes from curfew to cuddle with my new girl.

Here I was again, letting what I did off the field affect how much my coaches would tolerate from me on the field! It was no surprise when coach Embree confronted me about my lack of urgency as I exited the elevator on my way up to my room. Although it had been Embree who recruited me out of the Bay Area on behalf of the Buffaloes five years before, we weren't that tight.

I lumped him in with all the other members of the coaching staff I felt had tossed me on the side of the road. Our relationship was rather artificial, and as such, I met his confrontation with contempt. The decision makers were not pleased with me once Embree informed them of my lackadaisical attitude toward the rules. After finally getting into my room, glancing over my game plan one last time, I hit the bed. Little did I know, coach Embree and my little elevator confrontation was going to come back to haunt me in the near future.

I woke up early the next day and stuck to my usual routine. I grabbed the remote. Click. ESPN's coverage of College Football Game Day was on like clockwork. The ESPN crew was already talking up our pending game on television. To be honest, it always felt surreal to have our team be the subject of national sports news.

It was a beautiful day and as our team left the hotel and headed to the stadium, everyone had their game faces on and was ready for battle. Our team's dressing room was small and confined. This was a pretty smart design considering that it made us, the opponents, uncomfortable.

However, the rest of the stadium was so sick I couldn't believe my eyes. Truthfully, it made me wonder why some of my fellow teammates turned down The University of Texas to come to CU. This place made me feel like we were NFL stars. Not only did it seat 80,000+ fans, it also had breathtaking luxury suites, top of the line replay screens, one of the nation's best athletic training facilities, and a playing surface built for speed.

Thinking back on that day, I now realize that I was not mentally ready to play. However, the excitement of experiencing the top-notch venue made me feel hyped. They call football the ultimate team sport for a reason; it's because if your teammate doesn't have your back, then it could be the last play you ever make. You could hear the noise from the crowd through the doors of the locker room as our team huddled tight together to say a final prayer. It was time to test ourselves.

The doors leading to the field kicked open and we headed out into the deafening noise and the humidity of the notorious Texas climate. It was the first time we were face-to-face with the Longhorns, and each team matched the other's rowdy presence. As chance would have it, we won the coin toss and we deferred taking the ball until the second half. We kicked the ball off and went head-to-head with arguably the most potent offense in college football at the time. The Longhorns were made of names like Chris Simms, Roy Williams, Cedric Benson, and Derrick Johnson, to name a few. There were roughly 11 others who would perform as starters, or as back up on that UT offense, that would go onto have strong NFL careers. Needless to say, our defense was going to have their hands full that day, myself included.

As our kickoff squad was preparing to run out on the field, the last thing imaginable on earth happened to me. Coach Cabral, our linebacker coach, came up behind me, tapped me on my shoulder, and leaned over and yelled above the noise of the crowd into my ear, "you are starting in this game!" I remember looking at him with a puzzled look on my face as I felt my legs go numb after his unexpected announcement. Nevertheless, staring him dead in the eyes, I shook my head in agreement to show that I was confident and ready to execute his command.

Honestly, I should have won an Oscar for that performance, I was truly terrified because I knew I had not put in the work I should have during practice the week prior. I mean, this wasn't Chico State; this was one of the top offenses in the country. NFL scouts in the stands wanted to see which team was legit!

A variety of emotions came over me. How dare they wait moments before kickoff to tell me I would be starting? This could have quite possibly been the nightmare of a lifetime. Ill prepared, I scurried onto the field thinking to myself, "I guess I should have been careful what I wished for." My mind scrambled to make sense of this awkward decision. Nothing about the move was logical. I had been walking around our team's athletic facility all week with a bad attitude. I kept thinking that if I had known, I would have prepared like a starter. However, the truthful shame is that there should be no difference between how a starter and a backup approach a game. In a game as violent and reckless as football, I owed it to my team, and more importantly, to myself, to be ready!

All I could think about was what could go wrong for me in front of thousands of fans while on national television. When I ran into the huddle to join the starting defense, a few surprised faces stared back at me. They too wondered why I had appeared on the field with the base (starting) unit. It was just my luck that I happened to line up on the right side of the formation, against wide receiver Roy Williams. He would become the future #7 overall pick of the NFL draft, to the Detroit Lions in 2004.

The ball was snapped. Everything was moving so fast. The first play was a dive off of the left-hand side of our defense, for about a four-yard gain. We rushed back into the huddle, but it was way too loud to hear anyone talking on the field. Hence, in practice the week before we had prepared to communicate through hand signals. Looking at everyone's eyes after that first play was like looking at a bunch of deer caught in the headlights.

It wasn't long until the wheels came off of the wagon and the Texas Longhorns began to have their way with us that day. I personally gave up a 12-yard touchdown to Roy Williams early in the first half. I called myself trying to make a big play and sneak an interception off of the quarterback, Chris Simms, in the back of the end zone, when I saw him starring down his tight end. Unfortunately, he spotted me out the corner of his eye right before he released the ball and checked down to Roy Williams who had camped out right in front of the front pile on. My second mishap came in the 3rd quarter of the game. Of course we were in our predictable cover-2-zone defense, which Chris Simms picked apart all day. But on this particular play I made the mistake of not running with my man down the sideline long enough to give my safety time to get over the top of the receiver, before I let him go and the receiver crept down the sideline for a touchdown!

Just as quick as the coaches had decided to start me in the game, they had taken me out. Towards the end of the third quarter I got that infamous tap on the shoulder from coach Cabral. But this time I had come full circle. From starting in the BIG game, to being on the bench for the BIG game! Words can't express the amount of anger and frustration I was living with at that point and time in my career. As the game continued to reach its much-anticipated ending, I became more and more conscious of the fact that I managed to let a fabulous opportunity slip through my hands, as I sat on the bench starring down at the turf while the hecklers from the University of Texas had their fun with me.

Great coaches know that there are times when you have to give your players a chance to play through some of their tough breaks. In baseball, it's called letting the player hit through their slump. The only problem is in the world of Big Time Football, the industry is so competitive that few players get a chance to play through any slumps they may have. And ever since Gary Barnett signed on to be the head coach at the University of Colorado, it was made very clear that I was not going to be afforded that luxury.

We ended up suffering a 41-7 loss that day to Texas, which definitely confirmed to every player and coach on our team that we had a lot of work to do. And of course every team has a fall man, and in this particular situation, I was that guy. Embarrassingly, the blame for the staggering loss was solely mine. But realistically, when a team loses 41-7, a whopping 99% of the team is going to be responsible for that type of butt kicking!

The flight home that night was somber and quiet. It seemed as if the flight took twice as long. It's amazing how fast fortunes can change. Sitting on the plane heading to Texas I was told by one coach that if I had a great game I was going to make some money for myself. And now, heading home from Texas, I could not get one coach to look at me in the eye. I was disgusted with it! As the majority of the team and the coaching staff pondered over ways to put the pieces back together after our tough loss, I found myself sitting on the plane just wanting to get back to Colorado. I was overwhelmingly eager to wash away all my frustrations, disappointments and tears in some form of drugs or alcohol. It's a shame that I felt like that would help put a smile on my face.

CHAPTER 41

A Very Rude Awakening

I KNEW I was going to have to suffer a backlash for my personal performance in the Texas game, but nothing could have prepared me for the way I was treated and cast aside by our coaching staff in the following weeks. To be treated the way I was as a senior was not only embarrassing, but also very disheartening. Even though our team had suffered an emotional and physical loss to the University of Texas, it was essential that we didn't harp on our misfortune. We had to buckle up our chinstraps once again and travel down to Stillwater, Oklahoma, to face the Oklahoma State Cowboys.

We were very aware that we could not afford another blemish on our record, or our Big XII Championship dreams would be over. Even though I was not high on the coaching staff's "favorite people" list, I figured I would see a significant amount of time. Oklahoma State had a few different packages where we were going to have to use extra defensive backs and I counted on getting my number called again. Our Oklahoma State match up was the late game on Fox Sports that Saturday night, which was usually reserved for prime time games between big-time opponents. But Oklahoma State was a mid-tier team in our conference at the time, and the game was not considered a big-time game in our minds. We endured a hellish wait in a boring hotel in Stillwater, Oklahoma all day, until we loaded up our buses to go play a 6:00 p.m. night game. Since we had extra time to waste in the hotel, it was decided that we'd do a walkthrough of our game plan in the hotel's bottom level. There is no such thing as going over the game plan too many times as far as a coach is concerned, especially if that coach makes a lot of money! This was routine, whether it be in hallways, meeting rooms, or parking lots, the plays and scenarios would be drilled into our heads.

What wasn't routine was being pulled aside by one of my best friends and my teammate, Cedric Cormier, to talk privately.

"Hey T! I have to talk to you!" I followed him over by the elevators to talk. Cedric continued, "Dog, you're not even going to play tonight!" I gave him a look as if he was joking with me. Then he proceeded to say that he overheard our head coach, Gary Barnett, and my defensive backs coach, Tom McMahon, talking about our defensive backs depth chart going into the game that night. Convincingly, he said, "Look T, coach Mac and coach Gary Barnett were talking about the defensive backs and I heard them say, 'He's done. He had his chance. He's a senior and it's time we see what we have in our younger defensive backs...' Think about it T! We only have three senior defensive backs on our team who get any playing time and two of them start, Robbie Robinson and Michael Lewis. So McMahon and Barnett had to be talking about you!"

I stood there in front of Ced, in shock. Did Ced really know what he was talking about? I sure hope not, because if he was correct, that basically meant that my football career at the University of Colorado was officially over. I knew Cedric had no reason to lie. He was my friend. But why didn't this come straight from the horse's mouth? Why didn't my position coach or head coach pull me aside with this information. I put my blood, sweat, and tears into this school's football program. I was speechless, and extremely pissed off! I was able to eventually calm myself down and keep my composure. Our team would be at the stadium soon, for another Saturday of Big XII competition. I just prayed that I would have the opportunity to be apart of it!

CHAPTER 42

OL' Father Time

THERE IS ONE thing that no athlete, no matter how fast, big, or strong can escape, and that's father time. And every team plans in advance for the day when certain players are no longer on the team. They have to plan, because it's required for success. *Business* success! Whether it's a college coach who is desperately searching the high school and junior college ranks for the successor to his senior quarterback, or an NFL general manager who is expecting his star running back to retire within the next two years. All teams are planning.

In my case, I guess the coaches had figured that there was no upside in continuing to play me as a senior when they could develop a younger player for future years. The key is to try and never be compared with any younger players, even though it's inevitable.

I remember running out onto the field that night against Oklahoma State, eager to find out whether or not Cedric's prediction was going to be right. I should have been thinking about my assignments or enjoying the fact that I was blessed with another opportunity to play BIG XII football. But no, my mind was consumed with the politics of football.

Our team pulled out a late 4th quarter rally against Oklahoma State that night. It was actually a little too close for comfort. Our team managed to steal away a victory we didn't deserve by a mere 3 points. We played sloppy and uninspired football for the majority of the game. But our team was able to stay close and step up when the game counted the most. I personally couldn't care less whether we had won or lost the game, because my good friend Cedric's eavesdropping prophecy was indeed, correct. I did not have a part in one defensive play in the Oklahoma State game that night. Not a single play! I had started at cornerback the week before. And the week before that, I was the team's Defensive Player of the Week, but now I was reduced to only special teams. I found that my Special Teams production suffered as well, because I was often unfocused and uninterested. I didn't sign up with C.U. to be a special teams star! As a senior, or an NFL player in his final year of his contract, subpar ball is not an option because you will quickly be replaced.

After the game, as I undressed in the locker room, I found myself in a very dark place emotionally. It was the first time that I found myself pissed off that we actually *won* the game. My attitude was so ugly, and I reeked of resentment. I wanted it to be overtly obvious to everyone around me that I was displeased. Some childish logic in my head told me that if everyone saw that I was unhappy, they would be unhappy too. But of course that wasn't the case. It was the first time I didn't feel like I was part of the team. As Cedric walked past my locker, we just gave each other a look that said it all. You see Cedric was going through his own playing time misfortunes. Once respected as one of the fastest wide receivers to ever come out of the Houston area, he now found himself of little value in a predominant run offense. We commiserated quietly, knowing that we felt each other's pain. Many members of "Cell block '97" were hurting, but we also gained strength from the guys who were succeeding at the same time.

Our team gained a second wind after the big Oklahoma State comeback. We followed it up with a home win over a pretty good Missouri team, and then followed that up with a very strong road win against Iowa State. Unfortunately, my fate of zero playing time continued during our team's winning streak. It was amazing that our team was finally in a position to have a monumental showdown against the most prominent collegiate team in the division, the Nebraska Cornhuskers. It had been five long years of mostly lows, and a sudden rash of highs that positioned us closer to coveting the Big XII Championship. And our team was well aware of what was at stake!

CHAPTER 43

Nebraska Week!!!

RIVALRIES ARE WHAT *make* college football! Our game against the University of Nebraska meant everything. For our senior class, "Cell Block '97", this would be the game to define us, and we knew it!

The drama surrounding the game was intense and the entire two weeks leading up to the game were also intense. The task was very clear and direct; beat the #1-ranked Nebraska Cornhuskers in the final game of the season and receive a first class ticket to the Big XII Championship game at Texas Stadium in Dallas, Texas. Our team held all the cards. We had put ourselves in position to control our own fate. What made the task even sweeter was that the game was going down on Senior Day. We'd be playing for "all the marbles," during my final game at C.U.

Our senior class had been recruited to Colorado under the notion that every game against Nebraska would hold Big XII and National Championship implications. This had been a complete fallacy until my fifth year at Colorado. This would be the first and only game against Nebraska where it would indeed reign true. Our team traditionally had a bye week before the Nebraska game, and we would annually play the game the day after Thanksgiving. History between the University of Nebraska and The University of Colorado runs deep. So deep, that the color red is not allowed in the University of Colorado Athletic Training Facilities during the two-week period leading up to the Big game. This was a rule instated by and passed down from the lone National Championship Buffalo squad.

When I was at C.U., the Big XII Football Conference was shaped a little differently than it is now. Teams like Colorado and Nebraska have left the conference, and many new teams, such as Texas Christian University, have come in. But from the late 90's until about 2002, everyone in the Big XII knew that if they wanted to contend for a Big XII Championship, at some point in time they were going to have to stand up and confront Big Red, and the Nebraska Cornhuskers. So our team was very aware of this most formidable foe that stood in our way on the journey to our goal of a Big XII Championship.

I will give coach Gary Barnett credit for the fact that he was able to get the support of former Buffaloes around our team my senior year. One of the best moves coach Barnett made in 2001 was hiring Eric Bieniemy. As a former NFL running back, Heisman Trophy finalist and Colorado Alum, coach Bieniemy garnered a lot of respect from our football team. Coach Bieniemy never experienced a loss against Nebraska during his career at C.U. So Coach Bieniemy walked around with an air of confidence. His swagger seemed to increase with every mention of the Nebraska Cornhuskers. Many of the former Colorado greats came back and expressed the importance of our team winning the game. Great teams become great because the team reaches a point of exceptional accountability. When a team begins to play for each other, instead of for themselves, they become dangerous. And there is no better day to play for each other than Senior Day.

The week prior to the big game was electric. The level of focus in our practices and in our film room had risen to acute alertness and dedication as compared to the previous weeks. Our assistant defensive backs coach, Vance Joseph, told me to be very prepared to play in the big game. And in this industry, whenever a coach gives you a heads up, you need to make sure you are geared up. Our head defensive backs coach, coach McMahon, was experiencing rapidly declining health to the point where coach Joseph had taken over full control of our secondary, but of course, coach Joseph could always be overruled by coach Barnett at anytime.

Since the game was the day after Thanksgiving there would be no time to go back home for the holiday. My parents decided to head out to

Colorado, celebrate Turkey Day, and lend some love and support during my final game at CU. It seemed as if everyone had family in Colorado at that time. The gravity and importance of the game was such that the students didn't go home for their Thanksgiving holiday. Hence, tickets proved nearly impossible to get.

The odds makers had us as big underdogs at home, which meant not many people truly believed we could pull off a win. We were determined to prove them wrong. Nebraska was due for a fall from grace at the hands of the mighty Buffaloes. One thing an odds-maker can never account for are the intangibles. The fine print can flip the odds within a game. The intangibles are what usually cause 90% of the big time upsets you see in football. This could be anything from a coach sidelines switch, to maybe even an instance of a player talking too much smack about the opposing team to the newspapers. Whatever it is, the intangibles always have to be considered. In our team's case, the intangibles were a critical part of our upset plan. I had never played in a game that meant so much! Beating Nebraska after a 10-year deficit of loss after loss would be the dream of a lifetime. It would be a fabulous way to express my thanks and love to my fellow graduating senior class. If we could accomplish this task, then off we'd go to Texas the following week, for the final step in the conquest of becoming Big XII Conference Champs!

Once again, the game meant a lot. When you see guys so emotional that they are crying before the game, then you know that an explosive and magical performance is about to go down. There was no way that I was going to let my personal frustrations with our coaching staff affect me doing my job on this day. It was no longer about playing for myself; I was going to be ready in any capacity that my team needed me. This one was for my brothers!

Excuse me for saying this, but we didn't just want to beat Nebraska on the scoreboard, we knew we were going to do that. But we wanted to physically impose our will on them. The air was right for a major upset, and from the opening kickoff until the time expired on the game clock, we absolutely dominated the Nebraska Cornhuskers up and down Folsom Field. If the game were a grade school fight, Nebraska would have needed someone to pull us off of them. Regrettably for them, no one could, and no one did, interfere with the butt-whoppin' we handed them. This was a 62-36 drumming, which set a national record. At the time, this had been the most points ever scored on a University of Nebraska defense. We took out five years of aggression on the so-called #1 Nebraska Cornhuskers that night, and sent them back home hurt and demoralized. I even got a fair amount of unexpected playing time in our monumental win.

By the time the game clock had ticked down to 1-minute in the fourth quarter, there were already thousands of fans on the sideline just waiting to pour onto the field and officially celebrate. You could smell the liquor on their breath in the cold winter air, as they patted us on the helmet and shoulder pads thanking us for our service to the University. I would have frozen that moment in time if I could. It was what dreams and fantasies are made of. It was whimsical to see the crowd rush the field after the final gun... the goal posts tipping over... the looks of pure elation on my team-mates faces was almost too exaggerated of an experience to be a part of. I had become overwhelmed by what we achieved. This was pure pandemo-nium! This experience reminded me of why I chose to come to Colorado some five years prior. I had finally achieved what I came for.

Once the team finally fought our way through the hoards of fans and media and submerged into the locker room, that's when it fully sunk in what we had just accomplished. An astonishing display of emotions filled the room: guys crying, hugging, laughing, yelling, dancing, just pure joy and excitement!

By the time Big Vic and I had returned back to our condo, our answer-ing machine was filled to capacity. Message after message poured in from family and friends calling to congratulate us. Vic turned on the TV and the good news had spread nationally. It seemed as though every channel we turned to was reporting on our upset of the #1 Nebraska Cornhuskers. We settled on ESPN and relived the moment over and over again with every highlight they played. We didn't want the night to end and this was our way to bask in our glory. But, as the saying goes, all good things must come to an end.

The problem was that no matter how long we waited to beat Nebraska, we could not dwell in our success. We had only one week to prepare for our school's Big XII Championship debut. Our team had kept a replica of Texas Stadium, home of the Big XII Championship game, in our locker room since the beginning of the season, and it was truly a dream to think that we were about to catch a plane to experience the real thing!

CHAPTER 44

Going Back to Texas

NOW THAT WE were over the hurdle of the Nebraska Cornhuskers, our team had the college football world's undivided attention. Thanks to our late season winning streak, we were now labeled the "hottest team in college football" by many college football analysts. The way the Big XII south standings shaped up at the time, our team anticipated having to play the Oklahoma Sooners in the Championship game. Much like the Nebraska Cornhuskers, the Sooners forgot to compensate for the intangibles in their final game of the season and suffered a heartbreaking loss to their archrival, Oklahoma State. This meant that our team was destined to have another match up with our old friends, the Texas Longhorns. Not only did we have to play the team that drilled us earlier in the season, we would play them in Dallas, Texas.

The Big XII Championship game, designed to be played at a neutral location every year. The 2001 Big XII Championship clearly favored the Texas Longhorns in terms of geographic convenience. If no one thought we could beat Nebraska at home, then we definitely didn't stand a chance against our next opponents in their home state. If games played out like they were expected to, then there would be no reason to play the game.

We flew into Texas early Friday morning. Last week's events seemed as though it were a blur. There was no down time between the two biggest events of our college football careers. We could have used an extra week to prepare for this formidable adversary. Fortunately for our team, we began to get back to basics towards the end of the season, and as a result, we were playing our best football at the perfect time.

Later that Friday afternoon, our team had the opportunity to have a walk through in Texas Stadium. Goose bumps replaced the smooth skin on my arms as soon as the stadium was in view from my seat on the bus. I wasn't just a football player. I was a football fan! The opportunity to play on such a stage was truly a blessing. Every single one of us players was in awe as we took to the field for our team's walk through. Jerry Jones, the owner of the Dallas Cowboys, welcomed our team and congratulated us on our accomplishments when we arrived. He wished us luck, and then departed.

Also present were scouts on the sidelines eye balling our team. Each scout was measuring our physical frames in an attempt to determine whether or not we were suitable for their teams. Obviously, as a senior, my mind was consumed with the NFL scouts and player personnel reps that were in attendance. Here is a very simple formula that anyone who intends to play football can follow. Big games + big performances = big money. This was a fact that I'm sure every single player expecting to receive playing time in the Big XII Championship game that year was fully aware of.

On paper, it looked as if Texas should be able to dismantle our team with little effort. Their offensive line was big enough to be in the top five, in terms of size, for the NFL that year. They also could have formed a very competitive 4 x 100 meter relay team using the speed of the guys at their skill positions. To say that Texas was talented was an understatement. But talent alone has never won championships; it's the collective effort of the team that wins championships.

Our team knew that we had to play a near perfect game in order to have a chance at winning. We were most definitely going to need our fair share of breaks. The butterflies in my stomach were paying me a strong and lengthy visit as I was getting dressed for the big game. We were finally prime time, Saturday night, and on ABC. There was no way that my family and friends weren't tuned in to this event. As our team ran out of the tunnel behind our live Buffalo mascot, and into a myriad of burnt orange and white clothed fans, I caught glimpses of segmented groups of maroon worn by the Oklahoma Sooners fans who bought tickets in anticipation of their beloved Sooners being in the game. The smallest pocket of fans wearing black and gold were present at the far end corner of the stadium.

The game started much like our initial meeting with the Longhorns. Their offense went right down the field on our starting defense and scored on their very first drive. Of course not one of us Buffaloes will admit it, but everyone on our team was wondering if the Big XII Championship was going to look like a re-run of the beat down Texas handed us weeks earlier. Texas actually had a trip to the National Championship game pending a victory against our team. The Miami Hurricanes were already a sure lock as one of the contestants for the National Championship game. Now the rest of the nation was waiting to see the outcome of the Big XII Championship. Surely, most everyone thought the second participant in the National Championship game would be the University of Texas. Texas lead by three points mid way through the second quarter of the game. This was when the tide changed significantly. Our team was ripped apart by Chris Simms and the Longhorns offense in our first meeting because we were unable to get pressure on him. Our coaches were determined not to let that happen in the Big XII Championship game. They developed a fabulous defensive game plan. By mixing up different zone coverage with some well-timed blitz calls, our defense was successful at confusing the Texas quarterback. The pressure from our defensive blitzes forced Chris Simms to make some very dangerous passes. On one particular play, our young safety, Medford Moorer, got a good read on Chris Simms and made a nice interception on a crossing route by one of the Texas receivers.

The interception was great, but what happened after the interception convinced our team that we were destined to win the game. As Medford picked off the pass, he quickly cut outside towards the sidelines to race for the end zone. Two Texas players had their sights on, not only stopping Medford, but also putting a pretty good hit on him. One of the players was offensive lineman Mike Williams, the #4 overall pick in the 2002 NFL draft. His accomplice was running back Cedric Benson, a young freshman phenom who would eventually be the #4 overall pick in the 2005

NFL draft. As the two Texas players got right within striking distance of Medford, he made a last second cut back to the middle of the football field that sprung him loose for the TOUCHDOWN! It was a Big-Time play for young Medford and our team. But the play proved to be catastrophic for the Texas Longhorns. When Medford made his cutback to the middle of the field to avoid the contact from "Big" Mike Williams and Cedric Benson, it caused the two players to have a nasty collision and neither player would return for the rest of the game. We dismantled the Longhorns with Medford's interception, the touchdown, and the loss of two of the best players in college football. The Texas football team was devastated! Our team showed no mercy as we took advantage of their fragile mind state. Our offense pounded the football and our defense was able to come up with the critical plays we needed at the right time.

I think it was the middle of the third quarter when our team collectively began to believe that we could indeed become Big XII Champions! The Texas Longhorns were not going to concede easily, but when everything was all said and done, our team was indeed victorious! I have never experienced such a deep sense of team fulfillment before this night. We had accomplished something that no one expected us to do that year. To have a 3-5 record my junior year, only to bounce back to a 10-3 team my senior year, was truly the type of send off our senior class deserved. Our team went on to get slaughtered that year by the Joey Harrington-led, Oregon Ducks in the Fiesta Bowl. But our senior class had already signed off on our college careers after the Big XII Championship. With Colorado now in the Pac-12 conference, it's fitting that there will only be one Big XII Championship in Colorado football history, and that belongs to Cell Block '97! Certainly, we had spent too much time partying and being full of ourselves by the time we got to the Fiesta Bowl, to have a fighting chance at winning that game. It's a pitiful shame that we weren't prepared, especially given that the Fiesta Bowl was a big-money game that could have improved many peoples standing with the NFL. You never want the last game someone sees you play to be your worst.

My career as a Buffalo was officially over! Five years together, with plenty of highs and plenty of lows to last a lifetime, along with plenty of tears shed, and plenty of hugs felt. For the seniors, many of us geared our sights on having the opportunity to fulfill a lifelong dream of the NFL. The remaining underclassmen on our team would begin the next season as reigning Big XII Champions. Upon arrival to Colorado, our strength and conditioning coach said, "a class' legacy depends on whether or not they left the program in better shape than they found it". When Cell Block '97 arrived home, the Colorado senior class had finished second in the Big XII, so it felt extremely gratifying to hold my head up high at the end of my senior year and say we were number one. I was going to miss my teammates immensely, and I knew that the feeling was mutual. It would be the end of my young adulthood, and the beginning of my young manhood. It was every man for himself now; no longer could we lean upon the other teammates to shore up for the other. We would all be entering the open market, and in many cases, competing for the same jobs. A couple of my teammates already knew that they were going to be pretty high profile commodities in the upcoming NFL draft that year. As for myself, I was hoping for a late round miracle or a free agent shot in someone's training camp that year.

Every kid who grows up loving the game of football dreams of the day that he hears his name called during the NFL draft. And about 99% of the time, that dream includes their name being called in the first round of the draft. Even though I had made some amazing plays during my college years, I did not play enough plays for any team to pull the trigger on me early. It was just too risky for them to bank on someone who didn't have a proven, consistent record of play. If someone was going to extend me an invitation to training camp, then I had to have an amazing workout at our school's Pro Timing day in March.

Growing up in San Francisco, my childhood draft dreams always included me being drafted by the San Francisco 49ers. But beggars can't be choosers! Whoever was willing to cut a pay roll check was going to be my team of choice. All I needed was one opportunity! Whether or not I would be worthy would be determined by my dedication and persistence.

CHAPTER 45

Job Training

ONCE A COLLEGE football player's career is over, the next step is no different than the steps of the average college student who has graduated. It's time to find a job! But that's exactly where the similarities end. The mental and physical training that serious NFL hopefuls have to endure is so tedious and calculated, that it would rival navy seals training more than the average nine-to-five job. Thanks to the NFL's emphasis on pre-draft workouts, prospects and their trainers invest hours of time and thousands of dollars each and every year to prepare. Some top NFL prospects end up signing with the agents and management companies who they feel can get them the most money in the draft. Often times that also ends up being the person or company they feel can prepare them the best for the pre-draft process. Obviously, the top college players will be signing with established, big named agents. Conversely, the up-and-coming agents tend to gravitate towards the up-and-coming players.

The business of preparing for the NFL draft has gotten so big that athletes are often brought out to special training facilities and put through a daily regiment, replicating everything the NFL will put them through. Players who need to gain speed are trained to gain speed. The player who needs his off-the-field reputation improved, is prepped on questions the media and NFL representatives may fire at him. It is the first time many athletes learn to play the game within the game. You may ask yourself, "What game is this?" Well, it's the game of money! This is where they begin to learn how to get paid. The formula is simple. Figure out who cuts the payroll checks, find out what they like, and then go do it!

If the NFL is handing out checks and they like wide receivers that run 4.3 seconds in the 40-yard dash, then you know what you have to do. So, for serious NFL hopefuls, as soon as that last collegiate game is over, it is time to go to work! Guys have won and lost hundreds of thousands, even millions of dollars leading up to draft day, in correlation to their preparation. Right now I'm beating around the bush, so I'm going to get straight to the point. Guys are willing to do whatever it takes to get paid! Here's a serious question: would you be willing to do whatever it took to prepare yourself to go pro, no matter what the cost? Keep in mind your success on the test could secure a pretty nice future for you and your family!

CHAPTER 46

Time to Go Pro

I HAD BEEN competing for money for the last four years of my life, but the University of Colorado was the one flipping the profits.

I was very aware that I was going to have an uphill battle before any NFL team would put me on their payroll. The opposite was true for five of my teammates who received invites to play in the Senior Bowl that year. The Senior Bowl is the premier college football all-star game. I had my hopes on a back room deal to get into the East-West Shrine game. I played in the high school, Texas v. California Shrine game and my father's former college coach, Vic Rowen, was a prominent member on the Shrine committee who picked the players for the game. Unfortunately, when the East-West Shrine representatives sent a questionnaire asking our head coach, Gary Barnett, which seniors on our team were worthy of being considered for their all-star game, my name didn't cross his mind. Since I was not on the list of worthy Buffalo seniors, there was nothing my dad's former college coach could do for me. Again, I can't stress enough how important it is for you to be a professional regardless of what level you are playing at. Whether you are a high school kid, a college baller, an NFL hopeful, or a bona fide NFL player, it is a must that you are respectful and hard working at all times! My rude behavior and poor work ethic continued to haunt me beyond the physical reach of my college coach.

If I was going to get my shot at the next level, then I was going to have to catch a team's attention at our team's "Pro Timing Day." NFL teams have turned what is called "mining for prospects" into a science. No longer is a player judged solely on the merit of his college career stats, now potential prospects are put through a series of both mental and physical tests to determine their worth. When an NFL team is considering investing millions of dollars into an athlete, it's a golden rule that they try before they buy. The more money a team is considering investing in you, the more money they will spend to make sure you are the right pick!

One NFL employer hired a former FBI agent to investigate one of my ex-teammate's lifestyle off the field. Why so serious a measure you ask? Well, this was no ordinary transaction. This would be their first round draft pick, and it was better to be certain now than sorry in the long run. This former FBI agent talked to teachers, students who took classes with this athlete, people he hung out with, and even scouted out where he went, and when he arrived home at night. That's how serious NFL teams take the process of building their team. NFL employees lose jobs over picking the wrong players during an NFL draft.

Today's NFL players know just how much weight is put on draft testing, so guys spend countless hours prepping and strategizing for the various tests they will go through.

We had about 2 ½ months between our last game and our Pro Timing Day. A handful of my teammates decided to sign with some pretty high profile agents. They were blessed to have daily workout regimens led by professional strength and conditioning coaches. My situation was less impressive, as I had signed with a very small agency out of Dallas, Texas and my agent definitely didn't have any high-priced strength coaches on his payroll. Usually my workouts consisted of me by myself, at the local high school track. I was going to have to take the "Rocky" approach to the 2002 NFL draft. I had become accustomed to the underdog approach by this time, as evidenced at my years at C.U., so I didn't mind. Being an underdog was never a problem for me; I got pleasure out of proving people wrong.

The problem I developed in college, that absolutely killed me when preparing for the draft, was allowing my self-discipline to slack. I was used to being in the program, and now that I was out of the University of

Colorado football program, it was evident that I lacked structure. Instead of relentlessly preparing myself for my one and only shot at my dream, I chose to procrastinate. Sometimes when people feel a sense of entitlement to something, they don't respect the hard work needed to receive it. Looking back on my preparation towards the 2002 NFL draft, I know now that I took it for granted. I took it for granted that the NFL was owed to me. I couldn't have been more wrong!

When the day came to perform, I felt ready mentally, but my body was not physically ready to match what I thought I should be able to do physically. I exceeded expectations in the bench press, with 13 reps of 225 pounds, and I jumped a solid 36-inch vertical leap and had one of the fastest shuttle times posted that day. Going into the 40-yard dash, I was actually testing very comparable to many of the premier cornerbacks in the country.

My agent came over to me before my 40-yard dash and let me know I had intrigued the Cincinnati Bengal's scouts and a great 40-yard dash could possibly slide me into the last round of the draft. Even though I didn't have a lot of college film for teams to watch, I had made some plays in my career that you would be hard pressed to find on any other prospects films. I spent my entire life being praised for my speed. So it seemed fitting that my ultimate dream depended on my speed. Forty yards in 4.4 seconds was the magic time. That was the time that could put dollars in my family's pocket! Being a smaller cornerback, without a strong college resume to fall back on, 4.4 seconds or faster was the only key that was going to open up the gates to an NFL career.

Each participant wore a t-shirt with their jersey number on it and we ran in order of our jersey numbers, smallest to highest. So we were very aware when it was going to be my time to run. Once I noticed there were only two people left ahead of me, I began to get really nervous. So nervous, that when it was my turn to get on the track, my legs felt as if they were rubber. I was tight and tense. A good measure to help you tell when someone pops a good 40-yard dash is that all the scouts and coaches will begin to talk and whisper right afterwards to compare times. "Number 23, senior cornerback, Terrence Wood!" yelled our strength and conditioning coach, Doc Kreis. It was Showtime! It felt as though all of the hours of confessing that I would be in the NFL came down to this very moment. Put up or shut up!

Thirty-two NFL team representatives were standing down by the finish line with their stopwatches in hand. I got down in my stance; said one last prayer and then took off! As I flew down the runway, I could tell something was wrong. I was pressing. I felt tight! Unfortunately my result confirmed my intuitions. I could tell by the look on my agents face as I crossed the finish line that I did not run well. Not only did I *not* run well, I had run an embarrassing time. I simply was not ready! The opportunity of a lifetime, and shamefully, I was not ready. I had spent years to get to that point in my career and I was not ready. I had no one to blame but myself that day and believe me it was hard to bear looking at myself in the mirror after such a huge disappointment.

We all proceeded to do drills on the football field after the 40-yard dash. Without the 40-yard dash time that I needed, no matter what I did on the field, it was a done deal! As I walked off the field in disappointment after our workout, I had to pass happy teammates who had improved their draft status with their performance during the workout. I was genuinely happy for them, but as for myself, I wanted to crawl under a rock. I wanted to get as far from our athletic facility as I possibly could. I didn't want anyone asking me how I did. If I were lucky, maybe someone would see enough in me to give me a second shot. But there was no way that I was going to be able to count on that, because one player's missed opportunity usually becomes another player's golden opportunity. And in the industry of Big Time Football, you usually only get one shot!

CHAPTER 47

Draft Day '02

MY DRAFT DAY reality was polar opposite to what I had envisioned when I was a young child. No lights, no cameras, and certainly no reporters. My draft day consisted of a day at my future mother-in-law's house, with salsa and chips. I always expected my parents to be right next to me on draft day, but there was no need, my parents were thousands of miles away in San Francisco. Why waste the money on a plane ticket if you are not getting drafted, right? RIGHT! Thanks to my sub-par workouts for the NFL leading up to the draft, the best I could hope for was a free-agent tryout.

My first feeling of gratification during the draft came when my first teammate got drafted. Commissioner Tagliabue walked up to the podium and said, "With the 21st pick in the first round, the New England Patriots select Daniel Graham, from The University of Colorado." A smile came over my face as I relished in the fact that the first member of Cell Block '97 was off the board. One of my brothers had just gotten blessed with his ultimate dream! More gratification came as other Buffaloes began to have their names called out during the draft telecast. My roommate, Victor Rogers, was drafted in the seventh round by the Detroit Lions, which I felt was a slap in the face considering his career in the Big XII. I'm sure he was aware that he lost significant value because of his bad injury rap sheet; nonetheless, I was proud of him.

Football athletes who don't get drafted may get their shot to make an NFL roster by becoming a free agent. It's pretty similar to becoming a walk-on at the collegiate level, or a temp at a large company. Basically, you have a long road to travel! As an NFL free agent, you are at the bottom of the totem pole. I am a firm believer that if you're a beggar you can't be a chooser. I was willing to take an NFL shot in any form or fashion that someone was willing to give it. Unfortunately, there were no NFL teams beating down my door. Not even one prospective phone call from a team was made to me that day. But I just couldn't believe that *no one* was willing to give me a shot.

That's when the most unexpected call came through to my future mother-in-law's house. Since I didn't want to be bothered with any phone calls while I was watching the draft, we let the answering machine pick up the call. The voice over the answering machine was very clear and distinct in tone in my memory bank. This was a voice that I had actually missed hearing; it was Rick Neuheisel.

I remember thinking, "WOW! He didn't forget about me. He really did care." I later became aware that everyone who was recruited in our senior class by coach Neuheisel received calls that day; which is actually an interesting distinction when you consider the fact that none of my coaches I had just won a Big XII Championship with called me that day. Needless to say, Rick Neuheisel's character and spirit, struck a chord with me that day. That call from Rick meant a lot! It was a fitting end.

CHAPTER 48

The Next Step

I ARRIVED TO an electric weight room once I got to our team's training facility the following Monday after the draft. Guys were excited about seeing their dreams actually come to fruition. It was interesting to see the transformation in guys I came to school with as 18-year-old kids, and now they were grown men in the NFL. A couple of my former teammates were men who were guaranteed to make millions of dollars! Even the guys who weren't due to make any large amount of money were extremely excited just to receive a shot at the next level. When you have a room full of happy people, it's never too hard to point out the hurt faces, no matter how much that person tries to disguise it. I was the one wishing everyone good luck, while personally dying inside.

Beside myself, there were two other former teammates of mine who figured they'd get an NFL shot, but for whatever reason, they did not. Some of the fortunate guys down played the opportunities they were receiving in the presence of those who were not as lucky. This exemplifies exactly why we were a good team my senior year. It's rare that you have a team that genuinely cares for each other. Remember, the best teams don't necessarily have to be the most talented. Just ask the '2012 -'2013 Los Angeles Lakers, with Dwight Howard. Top talent + no chemistry= a poor season.

I walked out of the training facility with my head hanging lower than it did on draft day. The guy's who had agreed to contracts with NFL teams would be leaving for mini-camps the following weekend. Mini-camps are the NFL's opportunity to get a sneak peak at their new toys before the real training camps start at the beginning of August. As for me, I'd be sitting back in my condo in Boulder, Colorado continuing to try and break into the NFL. There was a lot of anger building up inside of me as a result of my failures. For some reason there was a huge part of me that felt robbed. Maybe it was the hours of practice? Or maybe it was the promises of a true opportunity to play at the University of Colorado? I don't know, but I do know that I was extremely disappointed!

Luckily for me, my family is well known and well-respected in the football industry. Before I knew it, my grandfather was on the phone and had used his leverage to land me two individual workouts with NFL teams. Individual workouts are ten times more promising for the player, as opposed to workouts where there are groups of players. Individual workouts are very serious! The NFL doesn't take kindly to wasted time and money. So if you are an NFL hopeful and you manage to obtain a personal workout with a team, you must take it very seriously! This is an audition like no other, where only you can make yourself fail. There is no other competition on the field. All players should work as hard as they possibly can, leading up to their workout to ensure that they shine and are well received.

At the time of my workouts, I didn't truly understand the value of what my grandfather had done for me. He put his name on the line for me, and now the ball was in my court. After all, he wasn't just any body. He was an NFL Hall of famer. People took his word seriously. My college career was over. I had no coaches, or anyone else to blame for holding me back. The stage would be entirely mine. Once again, it was time to put up or shut up.

Everything I did to prepare for the individual workout would rest solely on my shoulders. The first workout was with the Oakland Raiders. Obviously, being from San Francisco and having my entire family within a 30-minute drive of Oakland, would be a perfect spot to get my first crack at the NFL. My childhood dream was to play for my hometown San Francisco 49ers, but I found myself quickly visualizing myself in the black and silver of the Oakland Raiders.

The late Al Davis had always loved my grandfather. He recognized my grandfather's talent when he watched him play high school football in

Washington, D.C. Davis then guided him to play for a small junior college called Coalinga, in southern California. He later awarded my grandfather a scholarship to USC. That move led to my grandfather becoming the **first black quarterback** in the PAC-10 Conference. Al Davis also bought the rights to my grandfather's contract after he retired from the Green Bay Packers, and went on to become an assistant coach with the San Diego Chargers. In my grandfather's day, coaches actually *played* on the teams sometimes. Al Davis didn't believe my grandfather was truly retiring, so he figured if my grandfather ever got the itch to return to football, then he wanted him to be property of the Oakland Raiders, not the San Diego Chargers! Everything was working out to my advantage. The Raider individual workout was to be in a familiar setting at C.U. I was ecstatic when I heard that the Raiders had chosen to have their Midwest region scout work me out! You may say, "What's so special about that?" The Midwest region scout was Dave McCloughan, a graduate of C.U. So it's pretty safe to say that the cards were in my favor.

Dave let me know pretty early in the workout that the main priority was for me to pop a good 40-yard dash time. There had been red flags raised surrounding my disappointing "Pro Timing Day" times. There are some teams in the NFL that are all about speed. Al Davis had a history of recruiting super fast players; he had even attempted to convert Olympic track sprinters into football players at times. He liked speed in most of his positions, and I, as a cornerback, would be no exception. It was ironic that the one thing that was my trademark for so long was now my biggest dagger.

My father once told me that he always knew that I would at least get an NFL free-agent shot. He would have bet the house on it! He figured that even though I was not getting enough playing time at the University of Colorado, someone would give me a shot off of the pure fact that I was fast. You would think someone with a pretty good track background would not have a problem with a 40-yard dash. Like a home run hitter who is in a terrible hitting slump, I ended up running 4.6 during my testing that day. Which is okay for a fullback or a tight end, but it will not get you one red cent as a cornerback prospect.

I had one scheduled NFL workout left, one last shot to take hold of my dream. Just like my first workout, this one held special value as well. This workout was with the Green Bay Packers. Just thinking about that opportunity still gives me goose bumps. This is the place where my grandfather's name is forever etched in the stadium! It would be poetic justice to get a shot with the Packers. Forty-two years earlier my grandfather had to bang his way into the NFL by making the roster as a rookie free agent. At that time, the Green Bay Packers were the only team who were willing to offer him an opportunity. And now the Green Bay Packers were the only team left in the NFL who was willing to give his grandson an opportunity.

This workout was not an individual workout. From what I can recall, there were about four other players that were going to be tested the same day. The Packers flew me out to Green Bay, Wisconsin for the workout. In earlier chapters, I emphasize how recruits need to pay very close attention to how much money colleges spend while pursuing them. Well, this stands true even more so at the professional level. Teams will spend money on players they are really interested in. By flying me out to Green Bay for a couple of days, the Packers were showing that they fully intended on making me apart of their team, as long as I held up my end of the bargain and impressed them during my workout. Everybody loves a feel good story. And that's exactly what the signing of Willie Wood's grandson with the Green Bay Packers was going to be.

Everything felt right the day I was due to work out; my body looked good, I felt confident and the Packers' player personnel reps were definitely pulling for me to have a good showing as well. I knew if I could at least run a respectable 40-yard dash time, I could ensure a contract with my field work. I prided myself on my footwork and ball-catching skills.

My father's best friend and former college teammate, David White, used to tell me, "As an NFL hopeful, all you want to do is get to the part of the workout where they break out the footballs." Players are constantly put through tests that have nothing to do with football while chasing their dream. You have the 40-yard dash, the shuttle runs, the bench press, the vertical leap, the standing long-jump and so on and so forth. A sense of relief and comfort replaces fear and anxiety once the workout finally gets to the point where you can actually use a football. It's the only part of the workout where a player has an opportunity to go through football drills that actually might mean something throughout the course of a game. Obviously, if you make it this far in the "workout," then it's also a great sign that the NFL team working you out is somewhat interested in you. When a coach takes out the football, it's the NFL's version of moving the job interview forward.

To give you an inside view of how the NFL picks their players, here's a brief synopsis. There are minimum workout requirements for each position on the field. The NFL spends countless hours comparing and contrasting player's workout numbers, as well as their body of work on the field. After the analysis is done, it allows the NFL to put a draft value on each player of interest. If a player can't live up to the proposed minimum workout requirements, most NFL teams will put a high value on your film. It better be exceptional! If you don't have exceptional film, there's no reason to continue because NFL teams will feel you will not be able to compete.

However, the one thing the NFL cannot test a player for during workouts is the heart and emotion a player puts into the game. This is a key component that makes the not so gifted and talented great! How do you explain those great playmakers that may not be the fastest, or may not be the strongest, but always end up on top? In some instances an extreme amount of talent can count against someone because they may feel that they do not have to work as hard as others. While the less talented athlete knows that there will be no success for him without a relentless pursuit to work harder than all of his competition; for example, Jerry Rice.

The Packers had a beautiful indoor facility in which we were scheduled to run 40-yard dashes in that day. With great confidence, I had lacked in other tryouts, I thought to myself, "This is going to be the day." I had such a strong feeling that my lifelong dream of signing an NFL contract was going to come true! I was slated to run third out of the group. The artificial surface in the facility felt extremely fast to me as I warmed up. As I continued to prepare, I made one critical mistake that many athletes tend to make during workouts. I began to focus on the other players' performances instead of concentrating on my own preparation. Once it was my time to run, my muscles were not loose enough, and I popped my hamstring! Every player's worst nightmare involves injury. And I had just suffered my worst injury, during my most critical workout.

I was helped from the turf by a couple of players and limped into the Packers' athletic training area off to the side of the field. From there I was able to view the other players finishing their workouts. I felt sick to my stomach! Having to sit and watch while everyone else competed for contracts was actually more painful than my hamstring. I knew my entire family would be waiting by the phone that day in anticipation of hearing me say that I signed with the Green Bay Packers. But those would not be the words coming out of my mouth that day. As a matter of fact, I waited until later that night to give my family a call. Which, thinking back, probably indicated to my family that I did not get the job.

To make matters worse, I blew through two fabulous opportunities my grandfather gift-wrapped for me. I had never been known as a quitter, but I would be lying if I said that it didn't cross my mind as I limped my way though the Packers facility on my way out to catch my flight. I felt like my dreams had turned into my nightmares and I desperately wanted someone to wake me up! I had nothing left on my plate. The NFL season was right around the corner and I was still unsigned, and now critically injured. All I could think about was the amount of rehab I was going to have to endure to get my hamstring back to where it needed to be. Even if an NFL team called me up for a workout, I was realistically at least two months away from being physically able. Both mentally and emotionally I was done.

The mantra I got stuck on was that things were not supposed to end up this way. This was definitely not the fairytale I imagined. Now, I had a serious dilemma on my hands. If I was going to continue to go after the dream that had consumed me for so many years, I was going to have to find an alternate route. I wasn't fortunate enough to get drafted and I wasn't wise enough to take advantage of my free agent opportunities.

The front door and the side door to the NFL were both now officially closed. If I was ever going to make my dream a reality of suiting up in the NFL, I was going to have to fight my way in through the back door. Lucky for me, there were three professional leagues at that time that the NFL would occasionally give guys a shot from: the Arena Football League,

Canadian Football League, and NFL Europe. These were all viable options for guys who wanted to continue their career, and possibly get a second shot. It was definitely going to be a road less traveled, but the gratification of succeeding through the journey was what I was bent on doing.

After much encouragement from my soon to be wife, family and friends, I decided to continue to pursue my dream. There is an abundance of people who quit pursuing their dreams too early and literally miss their blessing right before they receive it. It's like the old lady and the "slot machine" analogy. She spends all day putting her little quarters in the same slot machine only to get frustrated with her lack of winnings. She gives up and leaves and allows someone to come right behind her, put in one quarter, and hit the jackpot!

I figured I was due for a jackpot. I just didn't know when it was going to come. I decided to get back to work after my hamstring felt somewhat ready. I used my frustrations as fuel—to get every single ounce of energy out of my body that I possibly could. I watched as my friends flew out to their NFL teams for training camp that year. I watched them play in pre-season games on television and I watched as their lifestyles began to change and morph with their new profession. The fire to make it was definitely burning strong inside of me, but without the right opportunity it wouldn't matter. I was still young and I had played major collegiate football. If I could get some good film of myself playing at the professional level, then I would get another opportunity at the show. Time, luck and perseverance would dictate which NFL team would come around to giving me a shot, if any.

CHAPTER 49

Humble Beginnings

AFTER ALL MY countless disappointments, my ego was in desperate need of repair. It finally began to sink in that the University of Colorado's umbilical cord had been cut. I was in the "real world" now. I found myself in desperate need to get back on the field, fast! All I had known all my life was being a part of a football team. I did not know how to define myself professionally outside of this life. A football team regimen had become second nature for me, going to training camp was somewhat of a comfort zone. I had been in training camp every August since I was 9-years-old, and I felt lost without it. I needed to be a part of a team just to keep myself from going insane.

My first professional shot came courtesy of my very own uncle, Willie Wood, Jr. He was coaching in the Arena Football League for the Indianapolis Firebirds at the time of my departure from C.U. It was a bittersweet opportunity for me. I absolutely wanted a job. But at the time, I thought the Arena Football League was a league that was far below my playing capabilities and standards. However, the idea of finally getting paid cash for my services did turn me on. In college, the bills are taken care of, but in the pros, personal bank accounts are taken care of.

What I found once I arrived in Indianapolis, Indiana, was that my estimation of the talent at the Arena Football level was absolutely wrong! Not only did I come across guys that were just as talented as me, many of the players at the Arena Football level played at big-time universities and had stories very similar to mine. They too had opportunities in the NFL, but for whatever reason, did not make it stick. The Arena Football League provided a chance to continue chasing a dream for most of us. Also, to a certain extent, the Arena League became a nursery for the NFL to keep a close eye on potential prospects they still felt needed time to groom. During my career, almost half of the Arena Football League teams had a NFL partnership in some form or fashion.

For anyone who spends five minutes watching an Arena Football League game, it quickly becomes evident that the game is designed to showcase the skilled players in the league. This is due to all of the passing plays and wide receiver motion rules. Very talented big men are hard to find, which is exactly why all of the talented linemen in the country are either playing Big Time College Football or are in the NFL. But small, fast guys, who can catch the ball are a dime a dozen. And that's exactly why there will always be extremely talented highly skilled players who never end up having a true shot at the NFL. I have participated in NFL workouts and Arena Football League workouts where there were so many guys working out, and I was literally a needle in a haystack! We call those "cattle calls."

During my workout with the Indiana Firebirds, I was able to impress the coaching staff enough that I was offered a practice squad position. For those who don't know, the practice squad is usually composed of four guys who don't play in the regular season games, but they practice with the team and are being developed to play in the near future. The interesting thing about the coaching staff's decision to sign me was that they had a vote amongst themselves that my uncle had to be excluded from any decision making process, for obvious reasons. So I felt proud that I earned that spot with my hard work and talent, and not just as a favor from my uncle.

I was offered the practice squad position as the season was coming to an end. I believe the team had four games left on their schedule at the time. My girlfriend and future wife, Delisa, was back in Colorado, and was due to have our first son literally any day. With the birth of my first son looming any day now and some discrepancies on when the Firebirds could start paying me, it turned out to be a poor fit. I ended up not signing with the Indianapolis Firebirds that day.

After that experience, I went on to bounce around between the Arena 2 Football League (the Arena Football Developmental League), the actual Arena Football League, the Canadian Football League, and numerous NFL workouts, before I decided to finally hang up my cleats.

The only league I didn't venture into was NFL Europe, but I was very close to heading in that direction a couple times. I was willing to play football on Mars if it meant I would get one more shot at living my dream of making it to the NFL. Luckily, I had a woman in my life that believed in my dream and my talent just as much as I did. Much of the time, she believed even more than I did. When an athlete is out of the university safety net, and fighting for a shot with a professional team, the support he receives is crucial to how far that athlete can go.

If a football player does not get drafted within the first three rounds of the NFL draft, most of the time he will find himself fully caught up in the roster rat race. Bouncing from team to team, and from league to league, trying to keep himself on someone's roster. I found myself enduring the roster rat race for the next five years of my life after I departed from CU. Competing against the same faces and watching the same guys get shots and lose shots.

It's interesting to hear the opinions of people who speak about the lifestyles of professional athletes; they assume it is stress free. The common sentiment is, "How hard can life be if you're making a lot of money and playing the Sport you love for a living?" Well, with fat paychecks come even heftier responsibilities and pressures. Not everyone who has talent or a dream is cut out to handle big responsibilities and big pressure. Many people crumble like a cookie under these huge demands. I know, because I did so repeatedly, and watched others do the same! God might have very well saved not only my relationship with my future wife, but he may have spared my life, by *not* letting me make it to the NFL. I know that probably sounds crazy, but I don't think I would have been mature enough to handle the responsibility of playing in the NFL. Always remember, having a good head on your shoulders, coupled with knowing what the pitfalls are, can help to secure your future.

CHAPTER 50

How the Game Has Changed

THE GAME OF football has never been the same since January 1, 1967. That was the date the first nationally televised Super Bowl game aired, in which the Green Bay Packers of the National Football League were taking on the Kansas City Chiefs of the American Football League. Ironically, my grandfather was playing in the game and ended up recording the **first** ever Super Bowl interception, which is a record that gratefully my grandfather will always hold. Ever since that infamous day when the cameras were given their sideline passes to the NFL, there has been an increasing love affair between the game and the camera. Once again, Super bowl ratings are clear evidence of this fact.

In the beginning, players used to be accessible and hold off-season jobs to make ends meet. This is in great contrast to today's players who are considered celebrities, and their multi-million dollar contracts ward off any thoughts of having to work a second job in the off season. To what do we owe this change? How did the game go from humble beginnings to pandemonium?

The camera lens is a very powerful thing. And it's exactly what has changed football into the #1 choice of entertainment in the United States of America. Football used to be a fun weekend sport before the introduction of television. Once television got ahold of football, the game turned into a theatrical production. Now the game had drama! Now the game had suspense! But ultimately, the game is about money! Unfortunately, priorities can change for people when money is involved. Loyalty is usually harder to come by when big-time money is at the center of the business decisions.

Television introduced football to big revenue, and big revenue turned football into a very, very, lucrative business. The NFL and The NCAA are as corporate as it gets. In today's game, Vince Lombardi would have had a multi-million dollar contract, coached in a stadium named after some dot. com business, wore Nike clothing on the sideline during the game, and had a television show sponsored by a franchised sports bar. These drastic departures from what true football used to be are enough to make coach Lombardi spin around in his grave. No longer is it just about football. Now it's about branding and licensing. Now it's corporate!

Television exposed our country's thirst for football, which in turn has opened up the door to all kinds of ways for the NFL to generate revenue. Television was just the beginning. Now there is NFL clothing, video games, and various business partnerships. As crazy as it sounds, television took football from a mom and pop business and turned it into a conglomerate. Football is now a true business enterprise and every other sport is playing second fiddle by far in terms of dollars and cents! And television didn't just change football at the professional level; it has also had a profound effect on the game of college football. It is just as much of a cash cow as its father league. Remember, the largest American football stadiums in the world are found in college football not the NFL! And with the increasing coverage of college football recruiting on the Internet, there is a developing eagerness to see more and more high school football on television as well.

The evolution of football as big-time entertainment happened so fast that I sometimes wonder if it was too fast. There are enough smart business men in the forefront of the NFL and Big Time College Football that I believe the two entities will not only continue to survive, but continue to thrive as well.

Who I am concerned about is the athlete. I believe that over the years, the athletes were taught to concentrate on the game of football, but not the business of football. And what has happened now is that the game has left many of its players behind. Simply put, while the game has grown, the players have not. Yes, guys have grown in size, strength and speed, but not as people, and certainly not as businessmen. I am absolutely sure that the only way someone can survive and thrive in Big Time entertainment, and Big Time business, is to be equally big in character and person. Again, I stress, success is not found in becoming a Big Time athlete, it is found in becoming a Big Time person. All lessons I learned too late.

There is a stigma attached to the word athlete, and for good reason, given that most are plucked out of struggle, placed in higher education without regard for their education, used as mere pawns to generate income from the football field, and then transported into NFL fame and lifestyle. Guys like Pac-Man Jones, Michael Vick and Plaxico Burress didn't sabotage their careers on the field; they sabotaged their promising careers off the field. And the industry that they work within should also be responsible for some of the blame. I have always liked the legendary college football coach, Lou Holtz. After Holtz was inducted into the College Football Hall of Fame, what he said made me like him even more.

> "I never coached football a day in my life. I coached life!
> The life of a talented athlete is a very unique life.
> You would hope that the fast moving industry,
> That plans to exploit the athlete's talent, would also be
> Willing to prep the athlete for the things he will encounter."
> - Lou Holtz

There really is an urgent need to prep the athlete for the things he will encounter off the field. You must understand that this is a cutthroat business. You can improve the worth of your talent on the field by becoming someone off the field. Take every opportunity to become well educated at every juncture in your pursuit of professional ball. Develop your character and understand the business so that you are not left behind. Too many athletes have proved it, more than I care to mention, that your talent and work ethic will get you to the top, but only your character will keep you there.

CHAPTER 51

The Needle

I INITIALLY DIDN'T plan to talk about performance enhancing drugs in this book because it is such a touchy topic. But it's such a hot-button topic, that I changed my mind! The subject has been talked about over and over again, but the interesting thing is that very few have touched upon the true reasons why guys actually use performance enhancers. No athlete wants to use drugs. If an athlete is on top of his game without drugs, he is not going to start for fun. Athletes who use performance enhancers are athletes who have convinced themselves that they need it. Athletes who use steroids are athletes who are feeling inadequate in some form or fashion.

It may be an NFL veteran who is having trouble staying healthy. Or, it may be a young free agent, who wants to find a crack in the door. If you think about it, the best time for an athlete to go under the radar with performance enhancers is right before the draft. I must admit it has always amazed me how a guy can gain 20 or 30 pounds of muscle in just two months in between the January Bowl games and the March NFL workouts, and still get faster at the same time! But I'm not going to mention any names. Many athletes juice, and often it happens right before the NFL Combine. It's a character choice, but it is extremely difficult to show character in an industry that habitually lacks it. I personally never had steroids offered to me in college, but I think I observed the results of its use. Cliques within our team would occasionally suspect certain teammates and opponents who we thought were using illegal performance enhancers.

However, nothing was ever proven. The first time I ever had steroids offered to me was once I hit the professional level. This proposition occurred when I felt truly inadequate. I was playing arena football and had just hurt my hamstring again, and I didn't want the coaching staff to know. I knew that if the coaching staff found out they would have to replace me, which would cost me my job for good.

I was in my apartment trying to hold back tears of disappointment, and at that particular time in my life, I was seriously considering retiring. I had strained my hamstring, and unfortunately, I was very accustomed to hamstring injuries throughout my career. By the measure of pain, I knew it was going to take me at least two months to rehab. I was going to be done.

A very good friend and teammate of mine came clean after seeing me in such a devastated state. He sat down beside me and began to confess his steroid use. Admitting that he had been using steroids as a performance enhancer since he was in college and how he had enough available for me to take a cycle if I wanted to. He went on to list the benefits to my hamstring if I decided to proceed. My initial reaction to his offer was, ABSOLUTELY NOT! But once the severe pain and my dismal fate of losing my livelihood set in, I was soon asking consumer-like questions. His knowledgeable answers brought me from a staunch "hell no" stance, to riding the fence. Football was my passion and if I could alter my fate by doing a cycle, then so be it.

I asked him to show me what to do. We went into the bathroom and he pulled down the same toiletry bag that he had always kept in our bathroom. I had never thought anything of that particular bag before because my roommate had routinely pulled hair clippers out of it to cut his hair. However, this time, instead of pulling out his hair clippers, he pulled out a syringe package, opened it, and then pulled out a small brown vile. Now, I'm not particularly scared of needles, but I was definitely scared of this needle. It was the longest and thickest needle I had ever seen in my life! My roommate poked the needle into the middle of the vile and turned it upside down.

By that time the questions began to spout out of my mouth a mile a minute! How much do I have to take? Where do I have to poke myself?

Is it going to hurt? My roommate instructed me to stick the syringe in my buttock, make sure I emptied the entire syringe and then massage the part of my behind where I stuck the needle for the entire night. He warned that if I didn't, then when I awoke in the morning, it was going to feel like a horse kicked me in my behind! He exited the bathroom and left me to my own devices.

I must have stared at myself for a good thirty minutes in the bathroom mirror, going back and forth on whether or not I should use the steroid. This was something I had promised myself I would never do. But I was at a point and time in my career where steroids felt like the only viable solution. I needed my hamstring to heal in record time. I needed to make money! As I proceeded to inject the needle, I held my breath. I could literally feel the solution shooting out of the syringe inside of me. I had taken the steroid called, DECA. It's actually a steroid that I believe is given to racehorses at times. As I headed out the bathroom, I gave my roommate one of those "ain't no turning back now" glances and went in my room. He followed behind me, and advised me to stay hydrated and keep messaging my backside.

I woke up the next morning after taking steroids and it felt like I had the worst Charlie horse known to man, in my ass! I had to actually roll my way to my knees to stand up. But there was definitely a stark difference to the way my hamstring felt, from the day before. As a matter of fact, I didn't feel my hamstring at all! I remember that it was at that particular moment that I became a believer. It felt like my body was years younger and had no limitations.

People don't understand that only after you actually take the steroid does the real work begin. Steroids are not going to make you any bigger, stronger, or faster than you already are. You must put in the hard work to see results! We would do countless curls with our curl bar and countless push-ups and sit-ups in the house. I remember pushing my body to the limit in workouts and waking up the next day feeling like I hadn't worked out in weeks! What steroids allow you to do is recover quicker. Steroids can allow you to push your body to the limit every single day, without ever having a hitch in your step.

Picture this: no matter how hard you run or how hard you lift, you have a body that constantly wants to do more. Steroids make it possible for you to work harder than the next man.

But they will not improve your lack of talent. If you can't catch, you won't be able to catch on steroids. If you're a running back and you don't understand the pass protections, steroids won't help in that department either. But if you simply want your body to recover quickly from injuries, or just the daily grind of the sport, steroids will do the trick.

During the time I was playing in the Arena Football League there was no drug testing. So every steroid cycle we took was guilt-and-consequence free. I definitely felt faster and stronger on the field. My first Arena game after my first steroid cycle, I had 6 tackles, 3 pass breaks ups and an interception for a 50-yard touchdown that got called back because of a penalty. And I was supposed to have a shredded hamstring. So needless to say, I think the steroids translated onto the field statistically as well.

I'll be truthful. In that young state of mind that I was in at the time, I found myself wondering why I hadn't started taking steroids sooner. Listen to me very closely when I tell you this, there are certain programs that have risen from the depths of college football obscurity to the National spotlight under the influence of steroids. One school in particular became a surprise burden to our University of Colorado team for years. We were so focused on the University of Nebraska, when this other sleeper team just snuck up on us from behind. Back to my point! Many guys use steroids during strategic times in their careers. But almost always, it revolves around some feelings of inadequacy. They want to be better than what they determine is within their means. They feel like all that's needed is a boost. It may be a boost to rise up the NFL draft charts, or it may be a boost to fight off a nagging injury. Guys have relied on steroids for a long time now, and whether you believe it or not, it has always been prevalent in the game.

Like I said before, steroids are a character issue. We oftentimes find out just who we are when the going gets tough. Some of us stand by fate and what destiny has in store, while others try to alter fate through the use of illegal substances. However, you can only alter fate temporarily. Cheaters never win long-term, and in the end, all you have is your body. Torn up, used, and literally abused bodies on steroids may not feel pain now, but in the end, the pain will come knocking on your doorstep. Steroids are super band-aids for athletes who would otherwise be disabled and in severe pain. Not only does it allow you to recover faster, but it also masks pain.

Pain is your body's way of telling you that something is wrong. When you silence your body's mechanism for telling you that something is wrong, you're also decreasing the chance for true healing. In fact, it can lead to serious health issues in the long run. Anabolic steroids, for example, which are taken to stimulate muscle strength and growth, can cause the testicles to shrink and sperm production to decrease. Infertility, stroke, heart attack, depression and anger issues are a few of the known side effects of taking these drugs. Steroids may provide you the confidence and recovery you need in a slump, but it can't renew your health. So before you say "yes" to steroids or any other performance enhancing drugs, ask yourself if you would like to say "yes" to poor health in the long run?

CHAPTER 52

Bent and Hobbled

ON JULY 31, 2013, I went to Washington, D.C. to visit my Hall of Fame grandfather, Willie Wood. My grandpa and I had occasionally talked over the phone throughout the years, but it had been a while since we had last seen each other. I really missed my grandpa. The time had passed faster than the two of us had anticipated, thanks to both of our busy schedules. Whenever my grandpa traveled from the east coast to visit my family, I was usually somewhere else playing football. And every time my family went to D.C. to see my grandfather, it seemed as if I always had some untimely commitment. Since the last time we were face to face, things had changed drastically for my grandpa. For starters, my father and I were not visiting my grandpa at his home, as he was now in an assisted living community. His health had taken a turn for the worse. The most disturbing changes were to my grandpa's physical state. The man, whose NFL Hall of Fame induction helped inspire my career, was now the man who needed help to get out of his bed and get to the bathroom. My father had forewarned me about my grandpa's physical condition before we arrived, but I was still unprepared to deal with the state he was in, once I laid my eyes upon him.

It pained me so, to be in the presence of a man who was a GIANT but now somewhat regressed to infancy. His dexterity and quick wit had turned to mush. As my father and I walked into the room my grandpa's eyes rolled over towards the door. He recognized my father right away, but had problems recognizing me. Dementia is just one of his many ailments.

Although my grandpa is bent and hobbled, and has a disabled state of mind, he still commands respect and insists on dying with it. The respect my grandpa has earned is very similar to the respect that servicemen receive. It's the type of respect that people give you after you have paid some serious dues and sacrificed for others more than focusing on your own needs. What his determination and accomplishments have shown me is that gladiators definitely still do exist! The only difference is that today they wear helmets and shoulder pads. As glorious as it sounds to be respected and worshiped as a famed "football gladiator," it comes with a very steep price tag. Twelve years of bone jarring hits in the NFL during the 1960's is not going to help anyone age gracefully, and my grandfather is no exception!

My father and I threw around old memories from the past to help my grandfather remember his oldest grandson. His memory began to pick up as the day went on, but it will never be back to 100% ever again. Unfortunately, it was the first time in my life that I didn't want my grandfather's life! It shocked me to the core when my father and I joined him for dinner at the assisted living home and we actually had to help feed him. Even though he could not express himself, I could clearly see that my grandfather did not like being dependent upon other people's help for something as simple as putting a fork in his mouth.

When we chase our dreams we tend to look at the positives that come with the journey. But very rarely do we reflect upon the sacrifices. *The bigger the dream, the bigger the sacrifice!* You can count on that! This was something I didn't realize until after my journey was complete. After you hang up your cleats, you finally have time to reflect upon the journey. And more importantly, reflect upon the sacrifices. Too many to count, but every single one worth it! The game of football had given so much to my Grandpa, but it had taken just as much, if not more away.

I recently read a newspaper article in which the writer explained how looking at one of the greatest running backs in football history, Earl Campbell, reminded him of the violence in football and the wreckage it can leave behind. When the object of the game is to inflict your will upon someone, most likely the game is not going to be good for your body. Whether it's torn knee ligaments, broken bones, or concussions, if you play long enough, you will experience one, if not all. Now, I must admit medical technology today is far more advanced than it was in my Grandpa's day, but technology can't do much for that 50-year-old NFL vet who can't sleep at night because of the unimaginable pain he feels in his right knee that has already been surgically repaired three times. Nor has medical technology found a way to abate the other side effects of playing football he's experiencing, such as concussion-induced dementia and depression.

I often think about my college roommate, Big Vic, and wonder what his quality of life will be as he becomes a member of the silver hair club. I know that the eight surgeries he went through in college will come back to haunt him! The sad part about it is that Big Vic knows this too. As a player, thoughts about your quality of life come into your head every time you allow a doctor to cut into you. The small aches and pains that I wake up with in the morning are comic strips compared to the horror others will live through.

One of the more disturbing stories involving high-stakes football is that of Andre Waters, an NFL veteran of twelve years, who committed suicide by a self-inflicted gunshot wound. The scary thing is that when the pathologist studied Mr. Water's brain tissue, he determined that the football field helped contribute to Mr. Water's suicide. In other words, football had taken him emotionally and physically to a place in his life where he thought it would be best to end it all. Sometimes pain can be so intense that people will consider doing things they would have never considered before, like habitually using drugs and alcohol, or just ending it all. While the majority of former players have painkillers to get them through the tough times, suicidal thoughts still cross their minds when the pain is too much to bear.

NFL football is still somewhat of a young sport. The American Professional Football Association League was formed in 1920. Doctors are just now getting the opportunity to really evaluate the effects of the game on a man's long-term health, and early research results are not favorable.

No one likes to witness their favorite player grow old. Especially when it's your very own grandpa! He barely edges out Deion Sanders for me in that respect, by the way. The entertainment industry is an industry that definitely loves to see "new" talent. Once you are no longer "new," it's time to move to the side and let the next newcomer take his shot at the game. The problem with that business model is that you never get to see what happens to that **actor, musician,** or **athlete** once the curtains close, and they walk off of the stage. You never see how they age! Some succeed once the cameras and lights are turned off, while others find some of their darkest moments in life after the spotlight. The psychological withdrawals players go through after their careers are over can be quite debilitating. There is the camaraderie of many deep bonds made over many years that is lost. There is the glory, worship, and attention that fade away. There is a sense of loss in terms of identity when you've done football your whole life and are told that you are no longer suitable for the job. All former players experience some level of becoming a castaway. There is a feeling of meaninglessness and emptiness. Some pick up and go and start a new life, while others wither in all areas of their lives, psychologically and physically with only fleeting memories of what happened on the field. There is no getting old and riding into the sunset after spending an extended amount of time playing BIG TIME football.

Recently, the NFL settled a $765 million dollar lawsuit, involving over 4,500 former players. It is a start in moving towards supporting many of the guys who help make the NFL the conglomerate that it is today. Similar to Vietnam veterans, these players' bodies have been through immense trauma and they do not have the money to compensate for all of the rising medical bills.

Some former players actually need 24-hour assistance and do not have the money to afford that type of support. By no means do I want to turn this into a political book about funding for retired players, but after helping my grandpa eat his dinner during my visit, I sure felt compelled to touch upon the subject. An ESPN, "Outside the Lines" report once had a former NFL offensive lineman, Conrad Dobler, featured for a special report about retired players. Conrad Dobler played in the mid-to-late 70's for the St. Louis Cardinals and was considered a very physical player. Some actually considered Dobler to be a somewhat dirty player. During his interview, Dobler made a comment that absolutely blew my mind! He said, "When I run out of pain killers I am going to commit suicide". He further explained that this was because at that point, the pain would be too intolerable to live with. These are the very sacrifices that few aspiring footballers are aware of. If someone does not have the resources to get what they need, what options do they have?

You have to keep in mind that when you are no longer in the NFL, or a part of that college football program, you no longer have the medical support either. However, that's when players need the support the most! After you hang up the cleats and age starts to set in, quality medical attention is essential. The human body was not designed to take on the physical abuse and violence that the game of football delivers. And as I watched my father lift up my grandpa's weak hand, to give him another handful of his favorite jellybeans, I was blatantly reminded of that fact! It's not ethical to turn a blind eye to the needy, especially when the needy are the pioneers of our nation's most lucrative sport.

CHAPTER 53

The Business Athlete

THIS BOOK WAS inspired from the disappointment of letting my one and only dream slip right through my fingers. I would be lying to you if I said I didn't have regrets. But out of our regrets, growth is possible. Out of our disappointments, lessons can be learned. What one can't capitalize on today, maybe the next one can tomorrow. Out of the hurt from my own lost dream, I received a new _mission_. A new _destiny_! It's time for a change! No longer are the days of boneheaded football players and dumb jocks acceptable. Not only is it not acceptable, it is condemned! There is a new call to action for what I call, the "business athlete".

This is the name given to the athlete who takes calculated steps to ensure success on and off the field. The business athlete realizes his true potential and squeezes the life out of it until it cries for mercy! A business athlete is a leader. A business athlete understands the responsibility that comes with high favor. The business athlete is someone that has been groomed for the road they are traveling. The business athlete is not only aware of the game he is playing, but he is also prepared to thrive outside the confines of the game! Business athletes are not defined by the game of football. Football is used as a tool to catapult them into whatever they were destined to do in life. The business athlete is the athlete who has branded himself as the total package. The business athlete receives the type of respect that translates from the locker room, to the boardroom, from the post game interview, to the community fundraiser. The business athlete is someone who is well-rounded and influential in all circles of life. Business athletes realize that all of the attributes they have used to become successful football players are the same attributes that can be used to be successful in any area of life! The athletes who understand these truths find themselves living very successful and fulfilling lives long after their playing days on the gridiron.

Football has empowered thousands upon thousands of players the opportunity to have access to people and resources that they would have never had otherwise. But I have realized that there is no point of a good opportunity if you are not prepared to take advantage of it. The windows of opportunity to access big things in this world are far and few between. Many never get favor, many never get breaks, and the business athlete recognizes that. The business athlete feels no entitlement because he understands that people don't get what they want or even what they need, people get what they deserve! The business athlete takes nothing for granted and manages to stay humble when success sways in his favor. The business athlete takes pride in protecting his thinking and chooses very carefully who to associate with. The business athlete is someone who is extremely driven by pushing himself to the limit. He is accountable for himself, his team, and others who he has influence over. The business athlete is a label that will not be used for all, but will become the standard for the best! It's for the athletes who want to be challenged. It's for the athletes who want to leave their mark on this WORLD and realize that they can.

The time for the evolution of football players has come! As a matter of fact, it is essential. The pressure and the trappings that come with Big Time Football can test you in ways that you can never imagine. With the lights of the stadium comes the microscope of the media, and the perception that the media portrays is usually what people believe. Currently football players have not been portrayed in a positive light in the media, which puts a strain on the growth of the biggest entertainment cash cow in the world.

The business is not indestructible, and neither are the athletes who fill the stadiums. As I take a step back and think about generations of young athletes who aspire to be our country's next Peyton Manning or Adrian

Peterson, I wish you the best of luck. I pray for you. Those men have sacrificed tremendously to achieve that type of success. After dedicating nineteen years of my life to my first love, football, I have some insight into the road that you are currently traveling or about to embark upon. If you only grasp one thing from this book, please grasp this: there are ridiculous amounts of money and power being exchanged in this business. There is a magnificent opportunity for you to seize both, and extend that past your playing years. Just remember, once you get to a certain level, it's not a game anymore! It's big business and the best advice that I can possibly give you is to become a business athlete, and do it quickly!

Author's Note:

I have truly enjoyed writing this book for you. I pray you receive value from it, and can pass it along to bless the next young aspiring football player. Thanks!

CPSIA information can be obtained at www.ICGtesting.com
Printed in the USA
BVOW08s0339040814

361466BV00007B/140/P